THE TURING TESTS

D0270765

EXPERT
BRAIN TRAINING
PUZZLES

Foreword by Sir Dermot Turing

This edition published in 2020 by Arcturus Publishing Limited
26/27 Bickels Yard, 151–153 Bermondsey Street,
London SE1 3HA

AD008072NT

Printed in the UK

Contents

FOREWORD

Alan Turing's last published paper was about puzzles. It was written for the popular science magazine *Penguin Science News*, and its theme is to explain to the general reader that while many mathematical problems will be solvable, it is not possible ahead of time to know whether any particular problem will be solvable or not.

Alan Turing's work at Bletchley Park is well known: unravelling one of the most strategically important puzzles of World War II, the Enigma cipher machine. The Enigma machine used a different cipher for every letter in a message; the only way to decipher a message was to know how the machine had been set up at the start of encryption, and then to follow the mechanical process of the machine. The codebreakers had to find this out, and the answer was not in the back of the book. To begin with, they had squared paper and pencils, and they had to work out the cipher-machine's daily settings, using intuition and ingenuity. These characteristics constitute mathematical reasoning, according to Alan Turing, who was confident that there was no difference between the reasoning processes of a human provided with pencil, paper and rubber, and those of a computer.

Although they did not have computers to help them at Bletchley Park, with Alan Turing's help new electrical and electronic devices were invented which sifted out impossible and unlikely combinations and so reduced the puzzle to a manageable size. And the experience with these new machines laid the foundation for the development of electronic digital computers in the post-war years.

Computers are now commonplace, not only in the workplace and on a desk at home, in a smartphone or tablet, but in almost every piece of modern machinery. Teaching people computer skills and coding are now considered obvious elements of the curriculum. Except that this is not so, in all parts of the world. In Africa, access to computers in schools is extremely variable, and in some countries there is little or no opportunity for students to have hands-on experience of a real computer. For example, in Malawi, students may have only a 3 per cent chance of using a computer at school.

The Turing Trust, a charity founded by Alan Turing's great-nephew James in 2009, aims to confront these challenges in a practical way which honours Alan Turing's legacy in computer development. The Turing Trust provides quality used computers to African schools, enabling computer labs to be built in rural areas where students would otherwise be taught about computers with blackboard and chalk. The computers are refurbished and provided with an e-library of resources relevant to the local curriculum, and then sent out to give a new purpose and bring opportunity to underprivileged communities. The Turing Trust's projects in Malawi have since increased the number of secondary schools with computers in the Northern Region of Malawi from 3% to 32%. This has enabled thousands of students to start using these transformative technologies for the first time.

Thank you for buying this book and supporting the Turing Trust.

Sir Dermot Turing October 2018

To find out more, visit www.turingtrust.co.uk

Notes to the reader

The puzzles in this book are not intended for the faint-hearted, but are designed to challenge experienced puzzle solvers. They are graded in three levels of difficulty, with the puzzles in the third level being truly for experts.

Unless otherwise stated the quotes in the book are by Alan Turing.

DOMINO PLACEMENT

A standard set of 28 dominoes has been laid out as shown. Can you draw in the edges of them all?

The check-box is provided as an aid, so that you can see which dominoes have been located.

2	1	2	6	0	3	2
1	6	1	0	6	6	2
1	4	1	4	4	1	0
0	4	5	2	3	3	3
4	6	6	0	5	4	4
3	5	5	6	5	1	6
5	3	0	5	0	2	3
1	3	2	2	0	5	4

0-0	0-1	0-2	0-3	0-4	0-5	0-6	1-1	1-2	1-3	1-4	1-5	1-6	2-2
			✓										

2-3	2-4	2-5	2-6	3-3	3-4	3-5	3-6	4-4	4-5	4-6	5-5	5-6	6-6

HIDATO

Starting at 1 and finishing at 49, track your way from one square to another, either horizontally, vertically, or diagonally, placing consecutive numbers into the empty squares as you go.

15			12			6
18		20	11	23		
30	28			25		3
		27		49	1	
45	46	47	48	34		37
			41			36

8

SUM TOTAL

Fill each empty square so that every row contains ten different numbers from 0 to 9. In columns the numbers may be repeated, but wherever one square touches another, whether horizontally, vertically, or diagonally, the numbers must be different. Some are already in place.

The black squares show the sum total of the numbers in each column.

	6		8		1		7		5
4			1	2	5	6			0
	5		3			4		6	1
		9		1		6	2	0	
	1	0					8	3	
2	8		5		1				4
19	35	34	24	23	27	27	33	23	25

"He [Turing] used to cycle to and from work ... he would wear his civilian gas mask to ward off hayfever. This apparition caused some consternation ... some would search the skies looking for enemy aircraft and others would don their gas masks just to be on the safe side."

Sara Turing, mother of Alan Turing

NUMBER LINK

Working from one square to another, horizontally or vertically (never diagonally), draw single continuous paths to pair up each set of two matching numbers.

No line may cross another, none may travel through any square containing a number, and every square must be visited just once.

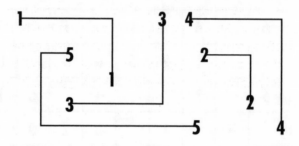

				8	18				11
8	4	3					12		12
5			18	2			13		13
						11	14		
			6	3				2	14
		6	17						17
		1							
5	4				10		15	7	
10			9			1	9		
16				16				7	15

LIGHT UP

Place circles (representing light bulbs) in some of the empty squares,
in such a way that no two bulbs shine on each other, until every
square of the grid is lit up. A bulb sends rays of light horizontally
and vertically, illuminating its entire row and column unless its
light is blocked by a black cell.

Some black cells contain numbers, indicating how many light bulbs
are in adjacent squares either immediately above, below, to the
right, or to the left. Bulbs placed diagonally adjacent to a numbered
cell do not contribute to the bulb count. An unnumbered black cell
may have any number of light bulbs adjacent to it, or none at all,
and not all light bulbs are necessarily clued via black squares.

SKYSCRAPERS

Place the numbers 1 to 6 into each row and column, one number per square. Each number represents a skyscraper of that many floors.

Arrange the skyscrapers in such a way that the given number outside the grid represents the number of buildings which can be seen from that point, looking only at that number's row or column.

A skyscraper with a lower number of floors cannot hide a higher building, but one with a higher number of floors always hides any building behind it.

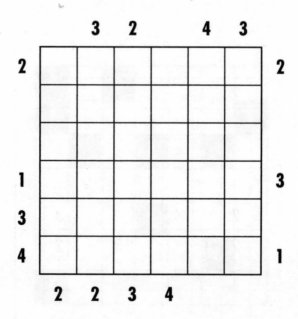

COIN COLLECTING

In this puzzle, an amateur coin collector has been out with his metal detector, searching for booty. He didn't have time to dig up all the coins he found, so has made a grid map, showing their locations, in the hope that if he loses the map, at least no-one else will understand it... However, he didn't count on YOU coming across the strange grid (as seen here). Will you be able to discover the correct number of coins and their precise locations?

Those squares containing numbers are empty, but where a number appears in a square, it indicates how many coins are located in the squares (up to a maximum of eight) surrounding the numbered one, touching it at any corner or side. There is only one coin in any individual square.

Place a circle into every square containing a coin.

	2							
1		1		2		2		2
	2	1	3		4		3	
						3		1
	2		4				3	
2	2	1			3		2	
		3				2		2
3		4			1		2	
	2							

NO THREE IN LINE

Place either O or X into each empty square, so that no three consecutive squares in either a horizontal row or vertical column contain more than two of the same symbol.

There needs to be as many Os as Xs in every row and column.

O		X	X			O	
				X	X		X
	O						
		X			O		
			O				O
	O	X					
				O		X	O
				O	X		

COMBIKU

Each horizontal row and vertical column should contain
five different shapes, and five different numbers.

Every square will contain one number and one shape, and no combination
may be repeated anywhere else in the puzzle; so, for instance, if a square
contains a 3 and a star, then no other square containing a 3 will also
contain a star, and no other square with a star will also contain a 3.

1 **2** **3** **4** **5**

LOGI-6

Every row and column of this grid should contain one
each of the letters A, B, C, D, E, and F.

In addition, each of the six shapes (marked by thicker lines) should
also contain one each of the letters A, B, C, D, E, and F.

Can you complete the grid?

E			A		
			F		D
	C	D			
		B		C	F
	A				

SHAPE SORTER

The grid below is divided into regions of three squares.
Some need to contain three different shapes: a circle, a square,
and a triangle; others need to contain three identical shapes.

When two squares share a side across a region
boundary, the shapes must be different.

CHAINS

Fill each empty circle with one of the numbers 1-7.

Every horizontal row, vertical column, set of seven linked circles, and diagonal line of seven circles should contain seven different numbers.

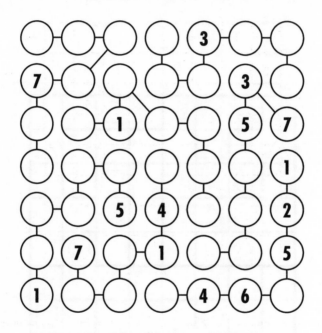

BRICKWORK

Every square should be filled with a number from 1 to 8.
No number may appear twice in any row or column.

Every brick that consists of two squares contains
both an odd number and an even number.

	7						6
8			3		7		
	4				5	2	
	6				2	7	
2		4	7	8			
	2	5			3		
3					4		2
		2				3	

**The Turing Test — discussed in Turing's article
"Computing machinery and intelligence" — sets
out the parameters for gauging a machine's ability
to demonstrate intelligent behaviour that is equal
to or indistinguishable from that of a human.**

14

PATCHWORK

Every square should be filled with a letter from A to E, and each heavily outlined set of five squares should contain five different letters. Every row and column must contain two of each letter.

Squares that share a common border may not contain the same letter.

E									
D			C					E	
			B			A		B	
		A		C					
			B		C		A		C
	D						E	A	
D		C	E		C				
C	D			B					B
	E				A		C		
	A	C	D			A			C

SLITHERLINK

Draw a single continuous loop, by connecting the
dots. No line may cross the path of another.

The figure inside each set of any four surrounding dots
indicates the total number of surrounding lines.

```
·  ·  ·  ·  ·  ·  ·  ·  ·  ·
   2     1  1     1  3
·  ·  ·  ·  ·  ·  ·  ·  ·  ·
 2  2  3  3  1  2  2
·  ·  ·  ·  ·  ·  ·  ·  ·  ·
 3     1        2  1
·  ·  ·  ·  ·  ·  ·  ·  ·  ·
          3     2
·  ·  ·  ·  ·  ·  ·  ·  ·  ·
    3        2  2  2  1  2
·  ·  ·  ·  ·  ·  ·  ·  ·  ·
 3     3  2        3     2
·  ·  ·  ·  ·  ·  ·  ·  ·  ·
 2           3     2     1
·  ·  ·  ·  ·  ·  ·  ·  ·  ·
                1        2
·  ·  ·  ·  ·  ·  ·  ·  ·  ·
 2     2  1  1        2
·  ·  ·  ·  ·  ·  ·  ·  ·  ·
```

21

CALCUDOKU

Each row and column should contain six different numbers from 1 to 6.

The numbers placed in a heavily outlined set of squares may be repeated, but must produce the calculation in the top left corner, using the mathematical symbol provided: multiply (x), divide (/), add (+), and subtract (−).

For example, when multiplied, the numbers 4 and 3 total 12:

12x	
4	**3**

7+	36x	20x		15x	
				2/	10+
1−		5+			
1−	15x	6/	3/	3−	
				2−	3/
2/		1−			

22

BRIDGES

17

Join the circular islands by drawing horizontal or vertical lines to represent bridges, in such a way that the number of bridges connected to each island must match the number on that island. No bridge may cross another, and no more than two bridges can join any pair of islands.

The finished design will allow you to travel from one island to any other island on the map.

```
   ①      ②            ②
③      ②      ②
   ①      ③            ④
③      ①

③         ⑤   ⑥   ⑤

②         ⑥   ⑥   ③
```

NO FOUR IN LINE

Place either O or X into each empty square, so that no four consecutive squares in a straight line in any direction (horizontally, vertically, or diagonally) contain more than three of the same symbol.

X			O			X	O		X
X			X					O	O
X	O		O		X		O		X
		O			X				
					O		X	O	X
			X		O				
	X				X	X		O	
	X				X			X	O
		X				O		X	
O		O				X	X		O
O	X	X				O	O		O

BATTLESHIPS

Can you place the vessels into the diagram? A number to the right or below a row or column refers to the number of occupied squares in that row or column.

Any vessel may be positioned horizontally or vertically, but no part of a vessel touches part of any other vessel, either horizontally, vertically, or diagonally.

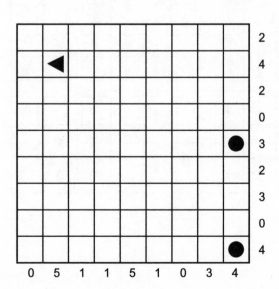

25

FUTOSHIKI

Fill the grid so that every horizontal row and vertical
column contains all the numbers 1 to 7.

Any arrows in the grid always point toward a square that contains a lower number.

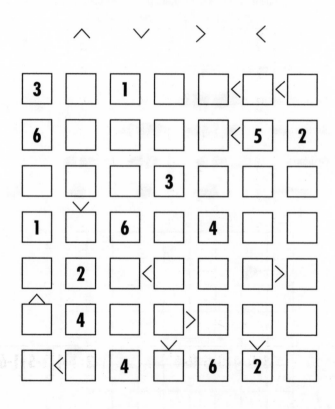

DOMINO PLACEMENT

A standard set of 28 dominoes has been laid out as shown. Can you draw in the edges of them all?

The check-box is provided as an aid, so that you can see which dominoes have been located.

5	1	1	4	3	6	3
2	6	4	4	2	2	4
0	1	1	5	6	6	5
2	6	0	0	5	0	5
4	6	3	2	3	0	5
4	1	5	2	0	2	4
4	0	6	3	3	0	1
6	1	1	3	5	3	2

0-0	0-1	0-2	0-3	0-4	0-5	0-6	1-1	1-2	1-3	1-4	1-5	1-6	2-2

2-3	2-4	2-5	2-6	3-3	3-4	3-5	3-6	4-4	4-5	4-6	5-5	5-6	6-6

HIDATO

Starting at 1 and finishing at 49, track your way from one square to another, either horizontally, vertically, or diagonally, placing consecutive numbers into the empty squares as you go.

	8			5		
10		12	6		1	3
21				16	15	41
	23	19	25			42
		26	37			44
30			36			
	29	35		49	46	

23

SUM TOTAL

Fill each empty square so that every row contains ten different numbers from 0 to 9. In columns the numbers may be repeated, but wherever one square touches another, whether horizontally, vertically, or diagonally, the numbers must be different. Some are already in place.

The black squares show the sum total of the numbers in each column.

5		4				7	0		
	9			8	0	2	3		4
2	4	6	1					8	
		9	5			6	3	1	
	6			7	3			8	
	9	7		5	0				3
20	**43**	**35**	**13**	**32**	**20**	**29**	**21**	**34**	**23**

"If one can explain quite unambiguously in English, with the aid of mathematical symbols if required, how a calculation is to be done, then it is always possible to programme any digital computer to do that calculation."

NUMBER LINK

Working from one square to another, horizontally or
vertically (never diagonally), draw single continuous paths
to pair up each set of two matching numbers.

No line may cross another, none may travel through any square
containing a number, and every square must be visited just once.

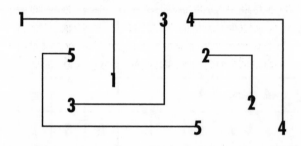

3					3				17
				8	6		5		
8	13	9				5		6	
14				13			9	4	
	2	18					18		17
		10		1			11		16
14				15	4				
					16				
2			1	15	11	7			
10		12						12	7

LIGHT UP

25

Place circles (representing light bulbs) in some of the empty squares, in such a way that no two bulbs shine on each other, until every square of the grid is lit up. A bulb sends rays of light horizontally and vertically, illuminating its entire row and column unless its light is blocked by a black cell.

Some black cells contain numbers, indicating how many light bulbs are in adjacent squares either immediately above, below, to the right, or to the left. Bulbs placed diagonally adjacent to a numbered cell do not contribute to the bulb count. An unnumbered black cell may have any number of light bulbs adjacent to it, or none at all, and not all light bulbs are necessarily clued via black squares.

SKYSCRAPERS

Place the numbers 1 to 6 into each row and column, one number per square. Each number represents a skyscraper of that many floors.

Arrange the skyscrapers in such a way that the given number outside the grid represents the number of buildings which can be seen from that point, looking only at that number's row or column.

A skyscraper with a lower number of floors cannot hide a higher building, but one with a higher number of floors always hides any building behind it.

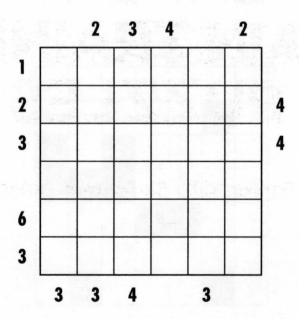

COIN COLLECTING

In this puzzle, an amateur coin collector has been out with his metal detector, searching for booty. He didn't have time to dig up all the coins he found, so has made a grid map, showing their locations, in the hope that if he loses the map, at least no-one else will understand it... However, he didn't count on YOU coming across the strange grid (as seen here). Will you be able to discover the correct number of coins and their precise locations?

Those squares containing numbers are empty, but where a number appears in a square, it indicates how many coins are located in the squares (up to a maximum of eight) surrounding the numbered one, touching it at any corner or side. There is only one coin in any individual square.

Place a circle into every square containing a coin.

	2		2		2		2	
	4			2	3			1
	2		2			3		1
					3	2		2
1	1						4	
		2		3				2
				4	4			
	2	4					5	
			3			2		

NO THREE IN LINE

Place either O or X into each empty square, so that no three consecutive squares in either a horizontal row or vertical column contain more than two of the same symbol.

There needs to be as many Os as Xs in every row and column.

O	X		O				X
			X				O
O				X		O	
		X		X			X
			X				
	X	X		X			
	X				X		

COMBIKU

Each horizontal row and vertical column should contain
five different shapes, and five different numbers.

Every square will contain one number and one shape, and no combination
may be repeated anywhere else in the puzzle; so, for instance, if a square
contains a 3 and a star, then no other square containing a 3 will also
contain a star, and no other square with a star will also contain a 3.

LOGI-6

Every row and column of this grid should contain one each of the letters A, B, C, D, E, and F.

In addition, each of the six shapes (marked by thicker lines) should also contain one each of the letters A, B, C, D, E, and F.

Can you complete the grid?

B	A		E		
	D				F
F	B				C
	C			A	

SHAPE SORTER

The grid below is divided into regions of three squares.
Some need to contain three different shapes: a circle, a square,
and a triangle; others need to contain three identical shapes.

When two squares share a side across a region
boundary, the shapes must be different.

CHAINS

Fill each empty circle with one of the numbers 1-7.

Every horizontal row, vertical column, set of seven linked circles, and diagonal line of seven circles should contain seven different numbers.

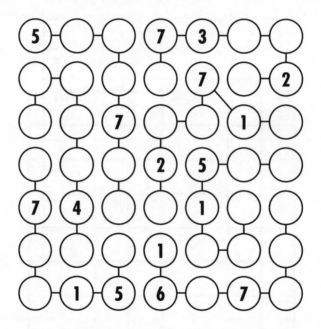

BRICKWORK

Every square should be filled with a number from 1 to 8.
No number may appear twice in any row or column.

Every brick that consists of two squares contains
both an odd number and an even number.

				1			
	3					2	7
			1		8	3	6
		8	2				
3	8			2			
	1			8	2		
	5					1	
4			7	6		8	

**There is a statue of Alan Turing in Whitworth Gardens,
Manchester. In 2012, the Olympic flame was passed
from one person to another in front of the statue,
on what would have been his 100th birthday.**

PATCHWORK

Every square should be filled with a letter from A to E, and each heavily outlined set of five squares should contain five different letters. Every row and column must contain two of each letter.

Squares that share a common border may not contain the same letter.

C		B				D		B	
E	C			A					D
C		D	C				A		
							C	E	A
		D							
		B	D	E	C		E		
	D		B	A				A	D
	A				E				
	D				A		D	C	
									B

SLITHERLINK

Draw a single continuous loop, by connecting the dots. No line may cross the path of another.

The figure inside each set of any four surrounding dots indicates the total number of surrounding lines.

```
·   ·   ·   ·   ·   ·   ·   ·   ·
      1   2       3   3       3
·   ·   ·   ·   ·   ·   ·   ·   ·
  2   1       1       2
·   ·   ·   ·   ·   ·   ·   ·   ·
      3           1
·   ·   ·   ·   ·   ·   ·   ·   ·
      1       2       2   1
·   ·   ·   ·   ·   ·   ·   ·   ·
    1           1   3
·   ·   ·   ·   ·   ·   ·   ·   ·
  3     3   3   3       0   1
·   ·   ·   ·   ·   ·   ·   ·   ·
  3   1       2       3   1
·   ·   ·   ·   ·   ·   ·   ·   ·
                          2
·   ·   ·   ·   ·   ·   ·   ·   ·
  3       3       3       3
·   ·   ·   ·   ·   ·   ·   ·   ·
```

41

CALCUDOKU

Each row and column should contain six different numbers from 1 to 6.

The numbers placed in a heavily outlined set of squares may be repeated, but must produce the calculation in the top left corner, using the mathematical symbol provided: multiply (x), divide (/), add (+), and subtract (−).

For example, when multiplied, the numbers 4 and 3 total 12:

12x	
4	**3**

1−		2/	18x		
10+	8+		30x		
			4/	13+	
1−	20x			10x	
		2/			
3/		3/		9+	

BRIDGES

Join the circular islands by drawing horizontal or vertical lines to represent bridges, in such a way that the number of bridges connected to each island must match the number on that island. No bridge may cross another, and no more than two bridges can join any pair of islands.

The finished design will allow you to travel from one island to any other island on the map.

NO FOUR IN LINE

Place either O or X into each empty square, so that no four consecutive squares in a straight line in any direction (horizontally, vertically, or diagonally) contain more than three of the same symbol.

	X	X		O		O		
O				X		O	O	O
O				X		O		
		X					X	O
	X			X	X			
X		X			X	X		
X		O	X		O			
		X				X		X	X
O		O			O		X		X
	O			O	X			
O		X	X			X		X	X

BATTLESHIPS

Can you place the vessels into the diagram? A number to the right or below a row or column refers to the number of occupied squares in that row or column.

Any vessel may be positioned horizontally or vertically, but no part of a vessel touches part of any other vessel, either horizontally, vertically, or diagonally.

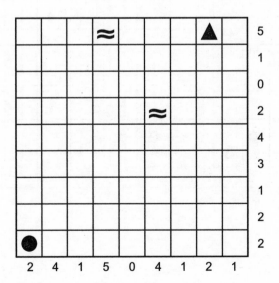

45

FUTOSHIKI

Fill the grid so that every horizontal row and vertical
column contains all the numbers 1 to 7.

Any arrows in the grid always point toward a square that contains a lower number.

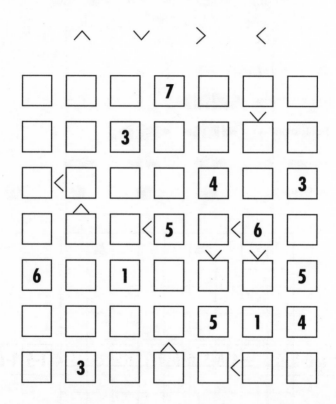

DOMINO PLACEMENT

A standard set of 28 dominoes has been laid out as shown. Can you draw in the edges of them all?

The check-box is provided as an aid, so that you can see which dominoes have been located.

5	6	0	6	3	2	2
6	1	0	2	0	5	4
4	4	3	5	5	3	0
0	2	2	1	6	1	1
1	6	0	1	4	3	2
5	5	0	4	4	3	4
6	3	5	4	5	1	2
6	3	0	3	6	2	1

0-0	0-1	0-2	0-3	0-4	0-5	0-6	1-1	1-2	1-3	1-4	1-5	1-6	2-2

2-3	2-4	2-5	2-6	3-3	3-4	3-5	3-6	4-4	4-5	4-6	5-5	5-6	6-6
					✓								

HIDATO

Starting at 1 and finishing at 49, track your way from one square
to another, either horizontally, vertically, or diagonally, placing
consecutive numbers into the empty squares as you go.

			26	24		47
32	30	29		49	23	
				41	22	
	4		40			44
	5		10	20	19	
	6	11				17
1				13		16

SUM TOTAL

Fill each empty square so that every row contains ten different numbers from 0 to 9. In columns the numbers may be repeated, but wherever one square touches another, whether horizontally, vertically, or diagonally, the numbers must be different. Some are already in place.

The black squares show the sum total of the numbers in each column.

		4		8	5		7	2	3
3				9	6	0			4
	8		4			7		1	3
	7				4		3		5
3	9		7		2				
2	8			9			4	6	
15	**45**	**16**	**20**	**43**	**29**	**26**	**33**	**27**	**16**

"*I have always thought Alan and his friend Christopher Morcom were the two most brilliant boys I have ever taught.*"

A.J.P. Andrews, Science master at Sherborne School

NUMBER LINK

Working from one square to another, horizontally or vertically (never diagonally), draw single continuous paths to pair up each set of two matching numbers.

No line may cross another, none may travel through any square containing a number, and every square must be visited just once.

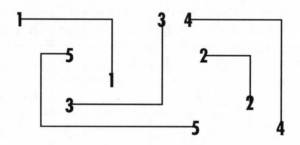

					3	10		
1			6	1	8			
		3			13			
	16				16	13	8	
6	9		9					10
17				4	7		7	4	14
		18		17	11			
18	2				2	12		14
				5	15			11
5	15							12

LIGHT UP

45

Place circles (representing light bulbs) in some of the empty squares, in such a way that no two bulbs shine on each other, until every square of the grid is lit up. A bulb sends rays of light horizontally and vertically, illuminating its entire row and column unless its light is blocked by a black cell.

Some black cells contain numbers, indicating how many light bulbs are in adjacent squares either immediately above, below, to the right, or to the left. Bulbs placed diagonally adjacent to a numbered cell do not contribute to the bulb count. An unnumbered black cell may have any number of light bulbs adjacent to it, or none at all, and not all light bulbs are necessarily clued via black squares.

SKYSCRAPERS

Place the numbers 1 to 6 into each row and column, one number per square. Each number represents a skyscraper of that many floors.

Arrange the skyscrapers in such a way that the given number outside the grid represents the number of buildings which can be seen from that point, looking only at that number's row or column.

A skyscraper with a lower number of floors cannot hide a higher building, but one with a higher number of floors always hides any building behind it.

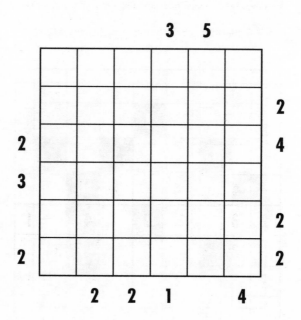

COIN COLLECTING

In this puzzle, an amateur coin collector has been out with his metal detector, searching for booty. He didn't have time to dig up all the coins he found, so has made a grid map, showing their locations, in the hope that if he loses the map, at least no-one else will understand it... However, he didn't count on YOU coming across the strange grid (as seen here). Will you be able to discover the correct number of coins and their precise locations?

Those squares containing numbers are empty, but where a number appears in a square, it indicates how many coins are located in the squares (up to a maximum of eight) surrounding the numbered one, touching it at any corner or side. There is only one coin in any individual square.

Place a circle into every square containing a coin.

	2			3		3	
2		2		2	5		2
					4	4	
	4		4		3		
2	3			2		4	1
	3	3		2		3	
2			1			4	1
		2				3	
1	2			1	1		

NO THREE IN LINE

Place either O or X into each empty square, so that no three consecutive squares in either a horizontal row or vertical column contain more than two of the same symbol.

There needs to be as many Os as Xs in every row and column.

X			X				
							O
	O						
			X				O
				X		O	O
	X						
	O	O					
X		O	X				O

COMBIKU

Each horizontal row and vertical column should contain
five different shapes, and five different numbers.

Every square will contain one number and one shape, and
no combination may be repeated anywhere else in the
puzzle; so, for instance, if a square contains a 3 and a star,
then no other square containing a 3 will also contain a star,
and no other square with a star will also contain a 3.

1   2   3   4   5

LOGI-6

Every row and column of this grid should contain
one each of the letters A, B, C, D, E, and F.

In addition, each of the six shapes (marked by thicker lines)
should also contain one each of the letters A, B, C, D, E, and F.

Can you complete the grid?

C		F	B		
		E	F		
	E				
	C				
	A			E	
D					

SHAPE SORTER

The grid below is divided into regions of three squares.
Some need to contain three different shapes: a circle, a square,
and a triangle; others need to contain three identical shapes.

When two squares share a side across a region
boundary, the shapes must be different.

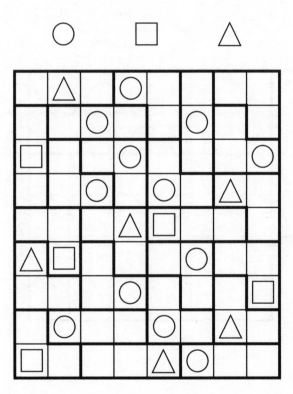

CHAINS

Fill each empty circle with one of the numbers 1-7.

Every horizontal row, vertical column, set of seven linked circles, and diagonal line of seven circles should contain seven different numbers.

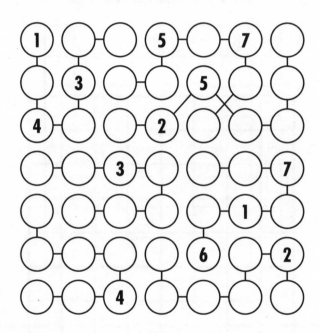

BRICKWORK

Every square should be filled with a number from 1 to 8.
No number may appear twice in any row or column.

Every brick that consists of two squares contains
both an odd number and an even number.

7	8				2		
		2	5				
	7				3		
	6					3	
						8	3
		7				6	
			2	1			
	5			8			7

**On the strength of his dissertation, in which he proved
the central limit theorem, Turing was elected a fellow
at King's College, Cambridge at the age of only 22.**

PATCHWORK

Every square should be filled with a letter from A to E, and each heavily outlined set of five squares should contain five different letters. Every row and column must contain two of each letter.

Squares that share a common border may not contain the same letter.

		A		C					C
		E					A		
C				D			B		A
					C			A	
D				C					
		B	D			D			B
						A			
D		B			D			C		A
	A				E				
C		A			C				

SLITHERLINK

Draw a single continuous loop, by connecting the
dots. No line may cross the path of another.

The figure inside each set of any four surrounding dots
indicates the total number of surrounding lines.

```
3       2  1                    2

           2  2  3     2     2

   2       2              1

   2       1              2

2       3     2  2  0  3  2  3

        2  1  2  3     3

   0                 2     1  2

1              2     3        2

   2  1  3           1     2

2  3     1        3  1  2

      2           3        3
```

CALCUDOKU

Each row and column should contain seven different numbers from 1 to 7.

The numbers placed in a heavily outlined set of squares may be repeated, but must produce the calculation in the top left corner, using the mathematical symbol provided: multiply (x), divide (/), add (+), and subtract (−).

For example, when multiplied, the numbers 4 and 3 total 12:

70x		7+	6/		28x	4−
			8+			
2/	1−	21x		2/		11+
		6+		1−	30x	
4/		12+				
84x	12x			15x		1−
		3/		7/		

BRIDGES

Join the circular islands by drawing horizontal or vertical lines to represent bridges, in such a way that the number of bridges connected to each island must match the number on that island. No bridge may cross another, and no more than two bridges can join any pair of islands.

The finished design will allow you to travel from one island to any other island on the map.

(2)   (4) (2) (2)

  (1) (1)

     (2)

(2) (6)   (4) (3)

(5)   (7)   (7) (6)

      (2) (1)

(3) (1)   (1) (2)

  (2) (4) (5) (3)

58

NO FOUR IN LINE

Place either O or X into each empty square, so that no four consecutive squares in a straight line in any direction (horizontally, vertically, or diagonally) contain more than three of the same symbol.

	X	X	X		O		X		X
O		X	X				X	X	
O					O			X	
			O	X					
	O						X		O
		O		O				X	O
O		O				O			
				O	O		X		X
	X		O					O	
				X	X		X	X	X
X	X	O			O				

BATTLESHIPS

Can you place the vessels into the diagram? A number
to the right or below a row or column refers to the
number of occupied squares in that row or column.

Any vessel may be positioned horizontally or vertically,
but no part of a vessel touches part of any other vessel,
either horizontally, vertically, or diagonally.

Empty Area of Sea: ≈

Aircraft Carrier: ◄■■►

Battleships: ◄■► ◄■►

Cruisers: ◄► ◄► ◄►

Submarines: ● ● ● ●

									0
								▲	**3**
									5
									2
									1
									0
									3
	▼								**1**
									5

0 5 0 3 0 3 3 2 4

65

FUTOSHIKI

Fill the grid so that every horizontal row and vertical column contains all the numbers 1 to 7.

Any arrows in the grid always point toward a square that contains a lower number.

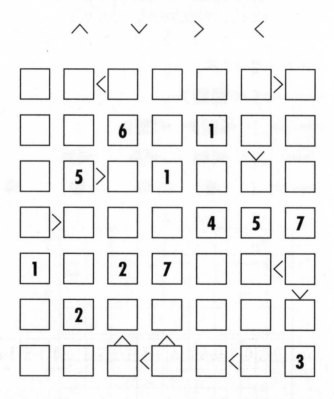

DOMINO PLACEMENT

A standard set of 28 dominoes has been laid out as shown. Can you draw in the edges of them all?

The check-box is provided as an aid, so that you can see which dominoes have been located.

5	6	5	5	2	5	0
2	1	3	6	2	4	6
5	2	3	6	4	4	1
1	6	0	0	2	5	4
0	4	3	0	1	0	2
3	3	2	1	6	5	0
2	1	4	4	4	1	3
0	1	5	3	3	6	6

0-0	0-1	0-2	0-3	0-4	0-5	0-6	1-1	1-2	1-3	1-4	1-5	1-6	2-2

2-3	2-4	2-5	2-6	3-3	3-4	3-5	3-6	4-4	4-5	4-6	5-5	5-6	6-6

HIDATO

Starting at 1 and finishing at 49, track your way from one square to another, either horizontally, vertically, or diagonally, placing consecutive numbers into the empty squares as you go.

	40		34			27
		43	36	32		29
	42			25		
18					49	47
19						
	1	5	14	8	9	10
2						

SUM TOTAL

63

Fill each empty square so that every row contains ten different numbers from 0 to 9. In columns the numbers may be repeated, but wherever one square touches another, whether horizontally, vertically, or diagonally, the numbers must be different. Some are already in place.

The black squares show the sum total of the numbers in each column.

			1		2	4	9	0	
4		9	3	8			2		
7	1			4	0	3	6		
8			3		7	1		2	4
	1	7		4				9	5
8	9					7			2
40	23	30	21	30	17	23	27	27	32

"He said that if the machine was liable to punish him for saying otherwise then he would say that it was conscious."

I.J. Good, Mathematician and Bletchley Park Cryptologist

NUMBER LINK

Working from one square to another, horizontally or vertically (never diagonally), draw single continuous paths to pair up each set of two matching numbers.

No line may cross another, none may travel through any square containing a number, and every square must be visited just once.

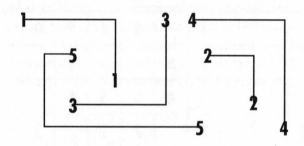

	1					13		8
3				7				
	5	11		2		2		
	3				9			8
7								13
		11						12
10								
					5	12		10
	9						6	
	1		4		4			
			6					

LIGHT UP

Place circles (representing light bulbs) in some of the empty squares, in such a way that no two bulbs shine on each other, until every square of the grid is lit up. A bulb sends rays of light horizontally and vertically, illuminating its entire row and column unless its light is blocked by a black cell.

Some black cells contain numbers, indicating how many light bulbs are in adjacent squares either immediately above, below, to the right, or to the left. Bulbs placed diagonally adjacent to a numbered cell do not contribute to the bulb count. An unnumbered black cell may have any number of light bulbs adjacent to it, or none at all, and not all light bulbs are necessarily clued via black squares.

SKYSCRAPERS

Place the numbers 1 to 6 into each row and column, one number per square. Each number represents a skyscraper of that many floors.

Arrange the skyscrapers in such a way that the given number outside the grid represents the number of buildings which can be seen from that point, looking only at that number's row or column.

A skyscraper with a lower number of floors cannot hide a higher building, but one with a higher number of floors always hides any building behind it.

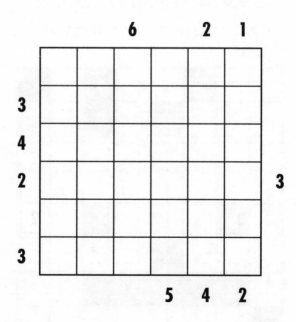

COIN COLLECTING

In this puzzle, an amateur coin collector has been out with his metal detector, searching for booty. He didn't have time to dig up all the coins he found, so has made a grid map, showing their locations, in the hope that if he loses the map, at least no-one else will understand it... However, he didn't count on YOU coming across the strange grid (as seen here). Will you be able to discover the correct number of coins and their precise locations?

Those squares containing numbers are empty, but where a number appears in a square, it indicates how many coins are located in the squares (up to a maximum of eight) surrounding the numbered one, touching it at any corner or side. There is only one coin in any individual square.

Place a circle into every square containing a coin.

1	1	1	2		2			2
	2				3			3
3		3		3		4		2
2					5		3	
3	3			4				2
		5				4		
3			4		2			2
	3			3				1
		1		2			1	

NO THREE IN LINE

Place either O or X into each empty square, so that no three consecutive squares in either a horizontal row or vertical column contain more than two of the same symbol.

There needs to be as many Os as Xs in every row and column.

						X	
O	O				O		
		O					
	O						
				X			
					O		
	O			O	O		O
X	X		X				

COMBIKU

Each horizontal row and vertical column should contain
five different shapes, and five different numbers.

Every square will contain one number and one shape, and
no combination may be repeated anywhere else in the
puzzle; so, for instance, if a square contains a 3 and a star,
then no other square containing a 3 will also contain a star,
and no other square with a star will also contain a 3.

75

LOGI-6

Every row and column of this grid should contain
one each of the letters A, B, C, D, E, and F.

In addition, each of the six shapes (marked by thicker lines)
should also contain one each of the letters A, B, C, D, E, and F.

Can you complete the grid?

		E		F	
					A
		B			
F		D			
					D
B					C

SHAPE SORTER

The grid below is divided into regions of three squares.
Some need to contain three different shapes: a circle, a square,
and a triangle; others need to contain three identical shapes.

When two squares share a side across a region
boundary, the shapes must be different.

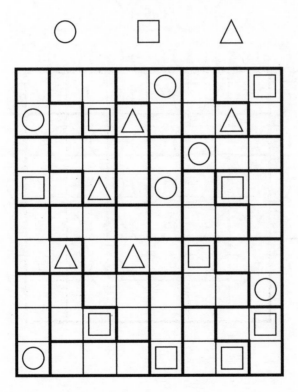

CHAINS

Fill each empty circle with one of the numbers 1-7.

Every horizontal row, vertical column, set of seven linked circles, and diagonal line of seven circles should contain seven different numbers.

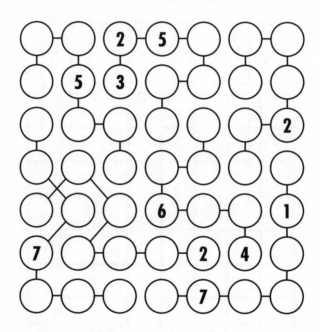

BRICKWORK

Every square should be filled with a number from 1 to 8.
No number may appear twice in any row or column.

Every brick that consists of two squares contains
both an odd number and an even number.

	7		4		3		
					2		5
	3			4			
			1	6			
5					4		
	6		8				
1			5				
6	2				5		

In 2019 the BBC held a public vote to find
The Greatest Person of the 20th Century. As well as
winning in the scientist's category Turing went on
to be voted the overall winner and greatest icon.

74

PATCHWORK

Every square should be filled with a letter from A to E, and each heavily outlined set of five squares should contain five different letters. Every row and column must contain two of each letter.

Squares that share a common border may not contain the same letter.

			C						
					E			B	
	A		D		B				
E		E		A				A	
D		C					E		
					D	C			
	D			E		B			
A								E	
		D	A				A	D	
D	E				D	E			

SLITHERLINK

Draw a single continuous loop, by connecting the dots. No line may cross the path of another.

The figure inside each set of any four surrounding dots indicates the total number of surrounding lines.

```
3   2       1               3   2
3       1               2   2   2
            0   2   3   2
        3           1   2               3
3       0           1       2   1           3
2               3   1   1   1   3
3                   2       2       0   3
2       3   3       2   1               3
2       2   2       3   2
    2   1       2       1       1   3
                3   2   2       1   3
```

CALCUDOKU

Each row and column should contain seven different numbers from 1 to 7.

The numbers placed in a heavily outlined set of squares may be repeated, but must produce the calculation in the top left corner, using the mathematical symbol provided: multiply (x), divide (/), add (+), and subtract (−).

For example, when multiplied, the numbers 4 and 3 total 12:

12x	
4	**3**

8x			35x	24x	21x	
10x					2/	
7/	15x	11+	13+	9+	3/	
						11+
2−			5+		8+	
72x				17+		
4−		3/				

BRIDGES

Join the circular islands by drawing horizontal or vertical
lines to represent bridges, in such a way that the number
of bridges connected to each island must match the number
on that island. No bridge may cross another, and no
more than two bridges can join any pair of islands.

The finished design will allow you to travel from
one island to any other island on the map.

(1)   (1)   (2)   (2)   (3)

     (1)   (6)   (2)

(5)   (7)   (5)

(2)   (2)   (3)   (5)   (6)

(1)   (5)   (3)   (2)

NO FOUR IN LINE

Place either O or X into each empty square, so that no four consecutive squares in a straight line in any direction (horizontally, vertically, or diagonally) contain more than three of the same symbol.

X		O	O	O			O	O	O
O	O		O	O			O		O
	O		O					O	
X	O	X					O		X
								O	
							O	O	O
X									O
	O	O	X	X		X		O	O
								O	
O			X	X			O		O

BATTLESHIPS

Can you place the vessels into the diagram? A number to the right or below a row or column refers to the number of occupied squares in that row or column.

Any vessel may be positioned horizontally or vertically, but no part of a vessel touches part of any other vessel, either horizontally, vertically, or diagonally.

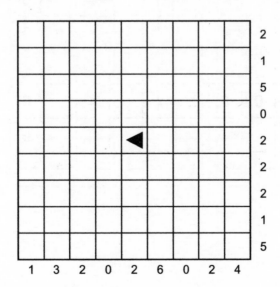

85

FUTOSHIKI

Fill the grid so that every horizontal row and vertical column contains all the numbers 1 to 7.

Any arrows in the grid always point toward a square that contains a lower number.

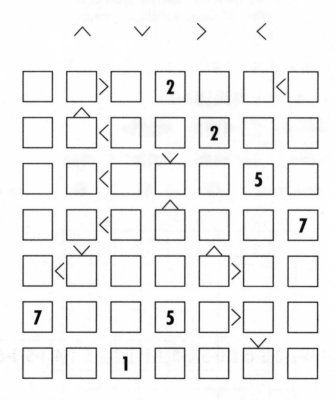

DOMINO PLACEMENT

81

A standard set of 28 dominoes has been laid out as shown. Can you draw in the edges of them all?

The check-box is provided as an aid, so that you can see which dominoes have been located.

2	3	2	2	5	4	4
5	3	6	1	0	3	6
5	3	0	3	5	2	1
2	0	0	6	0	5	5
4	4	5	0	3	4	5
2	3	0	6	1	1	6
2	1	4	6	2	4	1
3	6	1	6	1	4	0

0-0	0-1	0-2	0-3	0-4	0-5	0-6	1-1	1-2	1-3	1-4	1-5	1-6	2-2

2-3	2-4	2-5	2-6	3-3	3-4	3-5	3-6	4-4	4-5	4-6	5-5	5-6	6-6

HIDATO

Starting at 1 and finishing at 49, track your way from one square to another, either horizontally, vertically, or diagonally, placing consecutive numbers into the empty squares as you go.

28				32		
	23			43		
	25				39	46
			35			49
17		20	37			48
15		12	10	9	1	
	13				6	

SUM TOTAL

83

Fill each empty square so that every row contains ten different numbers from 0 to 9. In columns the numbers may be repeated, but wherever one square touches another, whether horizontally, vertically, or diagonally, the numbers must be different. Some are already in place.

The black squares show the sum total of the numbers in each column.

7		4			2		1		
	2		0		3	5			
	3	6							4
7					6				9
	9				3		4		2
3		6		5	2	1	7		
42	**25**	**33**	**15**	**33**	**25**	**11**	**20**	**28**	**38**

"From a very young age, I knew about the legend of Alan Turing—among awkward, nerdy teenagers, he is a patron saint."

Graham Moore, Screenwriter of *The Imitation Game*

NUMBER LINK

Working from one square to another, horizontally or vertically (never diagonally), draw single continuous paths to pair up each set of two matching numbers.

No line may cross another, none may travel through any square containing a number, and every square must be visited just once.

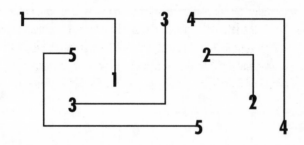

12										4
	11	12								10
	13				6			2		9
				10	4			8		7
5										
	11		8							
				3		6	2			
14		3								
			13					7	9	
	5			1		1				
		14						15		15

LIGHT UP

Place circles (representing light bulbs) in some of the empty
squares, in such a way that no two bulbs shine on each other,
until every square of the grid is lit up. A bulb sends rays of
light horizontally and vertically, illuminating its entire row
and column unless its light is blocked by a black cell.

Some black cells contain numbers, indicating how many light bulbs
are in adjacent squares either immediately above, below, to the
right, or to the left. Bulbs placed diagonally adjacent to a numbered
cell do not contribute to the bulb count. An unnumbered black cell
may have any number of light bulbs adjacent to it, or none at all,
and not all light bulbs are necessarily clued via black squares.

SKYSCRAPERS

Place the numbers 1 to 6 into each row and column, one number per square. Each number represents a skyscraper of that many floors.

Arrange the skyscrapers in such a way that the given number outside the grid represents the number of buildings which can be seen from that point, looking only at that number's row or column.

A skyscraper with a lower number of floors cannot hide a higher building, but one with a higher number of floors always hides any building behind it.

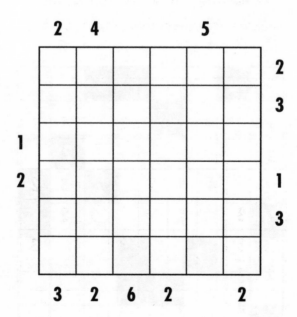

COIN COLLECTING

In this puzzle, an amateur coin collector has been out with his metal detector, searching for booty. He didn't have time to dig up all the coins he found, so has made a grid map, showing their locations, in the hope that if he loses the map, at least no-one else will understand it... However, he didn't count on YOU coming across the strange grid (as seen here). Will you be able to discover the correct number of coins and their precise locations?

Those squares containing numbers are empty, but where a number appears in a square, it indicates how many coins are located in the squares (up to a maximum of eight) surrounding the numbered one, touching it at any corner or side. There is only one coin in any individual square.

Place a circle into every square containing a coin.

			3	2		2		
1					2		4	3
2					2		2	
		4		5			3	2
2	3					3	2	
	3				3			3
2	3			2		4		
	3		4		3			3
			3		2		1	

NO THREE IN LINE

Place either O or X into each empty square, so that no three consecutive squares in either a horizontal row or vertical column contain more than two of the same symbol.

There needs to be as many Os as Xs in every row and column.

X	X			X			X
		X					
							X
O	O			X	X		
		X				X	O
	X				O		
		X					
					O		

COMBIKU

Each horizontal row and vertical column should contain five different shapes, and five different numbers.

Every square will contain one number and one shape, and no combination may be repeated anywhere else in the puzzle; so, for instance, if a square contains a 3 and a star, then no other square containing a 3 will also contain a star, and no other square with a star will also contain a 3.

1   **2**   **3**   **4**   **5**

LOGI-6

Every row and column of this grid should contain
one each of the letters A, B, C, D, E, and F.

In addition, each of the six shapes (marked by thicker lines)
should also contain one each of the letters A, B, C, D, E, and F.

Can you complete the grid?

	F				
				A	
E				B	
				C	D
		D			

SHAPE SORTER

The grid below is divided into regions of three squares.
Some need to contain three different shapes: a circle, a square,
and a triangle; others need to contain three identical shapes.

When two squares share a side across a region
boundary, the shapes must be different.

92

CHAINS

Fill each empty circle with one of the numbers 1-8.

Every horizontal row, vertical column, set of seven linked circles, and diagonal line of seven circles should contain seven different numbers.

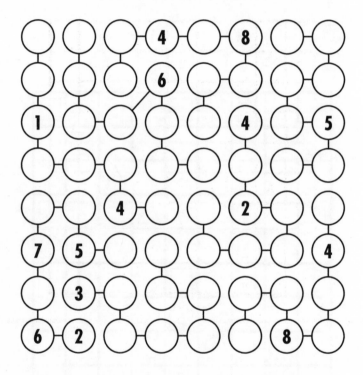

BRICKWORK

Every square should be filled with a number from 1 to 9.
No number may appear twice in any row or column.

Every brick that consists of two squares contains
both an odd number and an even number.

		3			1			
9				2	5			
		5	4				8	9
1			8			2		
					2			7
	6	1						
3				9			4	
	7				8	3		
			5			8		3

**Turing gave the very first known lecture to
refer to computer intelligence in 1947. He is
considered the "father of modern computing".**

94

PATCHWORK

Every square should be filled with a letter from A to F, and each heavily outlined set of six squares should contain six different letters. Every row and column must contain two of each letter.

Squares that share a common border may not contain the same letter.

			B	F		E		C			A
	A	D	C						E	B	
D	E	C		D						F	A
E		E			C			B		A	F
		A									E
			A	E	D		F		A		
		A	F	C						B	
						D	C	F	D		
	B			A	E						C
	F		E							E	
	B	E					B		A		
A	F	B								D	

95

SLITHERLINK

Draw a single continuous loop, by connecting the
dots. No line may cross the path of another.

The figure inside each set of any four surrounding dots
indicates the total number of surrounding lines.

```
.  .  .  .  .  .  .  .  .  .  .  .
    2     2  1     2  2  3
.  .  .  .  .  .  .  .  .  .  .  .
       2     2  3        1  3
.  .  .  .  .  .  .  .  .  .  .  .
 2  1     2           2     3
.  .  .  .  .  .  .  .  .  .  .  .
 2  1  1     3  2  3
.  .  .  .  .  .  .  .  .  .  .  .
 3              1  3     1
.  .  .  .  .  .  .  .  .  .  .  .
 2     2  1        2  1  0
.  .  .  .  .  .  .  .  .  .  .  .
 2     3     1     2        3
.  .  .  .  .  .  .  .  .  .  .  .
 2  1     1  2     3        1
.  .  .  .  .  .  .  .  .  .  .  .
    2  3              0  1
.  .  .  .  .  .  .  .  .  .  .  .
 3  2     1     2  3        2
.  .  .  .  .  .  .  .  .  .  .  .
       3     2        2  2
.  .  .  .  .  .  .  .  .  .  .  .
    2           3  2  3     3
.  .  .  .  .  .  .  .  .  .  .  .
```

CALCUDOKU

Each row and column should contain eight different numbers from 1 to 8.

The numbers placed in a heavily outlined set of squares may be repeated, but must produce the calculation in the top left corner, using the mathematical symbol provided: multiply (x), divide (/), add (+), and subtract (−).

For example, when multiplied, the numbers 4 and 3 total 12:

12x	
4	**3**

112x		10+	2−		9+		24x
	21x		3−	7+			
3−				15+	48x		2/
	6/		2/		11+	21x	
2/		5−		15x			
20x			11+		96x		
15+				12x		2−	35x
	2/		9+				

BRIDGES

Join the circular islands by drawing horizontal or vertical lines to represent bridges, in such a way that the number of bridges connected to each island must match the number on that island. No bridge may cross another, and no more than two bridges can join any pair of islands.

The finished design will allow you to travel from one island to any other island on the map.

NO FOUR IN LINE

Place either O or X into each empty square, so that no four consecutive squares in a straight line in any direction (horizontally, vertically, or diagonally) contain more than three of the same symbol.

	O	X	O	X			X	O	X
	X			O				X	
		X						X	X
O		X	X			O		O	X
		X					O		
	X			O				X	
					O				X
							O		
			O			O		O	
	X			X				O	
X			X		X	O			O
X					O			X	X
		O	O	X			X	O	X

BATTLESHIPS

Can you place the vessels into the diagram? A number to the right or below a row or column refers to the number of occupied squares in that row or column.

Any vessel may be positioned horizontally or vertically, but no part of a vessel touches part of any other vessel, either horizontally, vertically, or diagonally.

Empty Area of Sea: ≈

Aircraft Carrier: ◄■■►

Battleships: ◄■► ◄■■►

Cruisers: ◄► ◄► ◄►

Submarines: ● ● ● ●

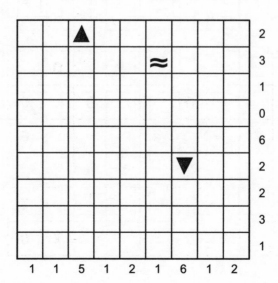

FUTOSHIKI

Fill the grid so that every horizontal row and vertical
column contains all the numbers 1 to 8.

Any arrows in the grid always point toward a square that contains a lower number.

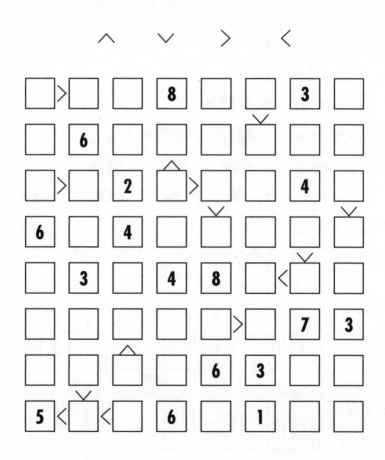

DOMINO PLACEMENT

A set of 36 dominoes has been laid out as shown.
Can you draw in the edges of them all?

The check-box is provided as an aid, so that you can
see which dominoes have been located.

1	7	1	6	3	1	0	0
0	2	5	4	5	6	7	1
1	0	6	7	5	3	3	1
4	3	6	2	5	4	2	3
5	1	3	7	6	4	6	2
1	4	1	2	7	0	6	0
6	4	5	3	7	7	2	3
7	0	5	5	7	0	0	4
4	3	4	2	6	2	2	5

0-0	0-1	0-2	0-3	0-4	0-5	0-6	0-7	1-1	1-2	1-3	1-4

1-5	1-6	1-7	2-2	2-3	2-4	2-5	2-6	2-7	3-3	3-4	3-5

3-6	3-7	4-4	4-5	4-6	4-7	5-5	5-6	5-7	6-6	6-7	7-7

HIDATO

Starting at 1 and finishing at 64, track your way from one square to another, either horizontally, vertically, or diagonally, placing consecutive numbers into the empty squares as you go.

34			29			13	
32						10	12
	31				6		19
	25			5	16	20	
	2		51			64	61
1		49		52		62	
40	42	45	48		56	57	
	43					55	

SUM TOTAL

Fill each empty square so that every row contains ten different numbers
from 0 to 9. In columns the numbers may be repeated, but wherever one
square touches another, whether horizontally, vertically, or diagonally,
the numbers must be different. Some are already in place.

The black squares show the sum total of the numbers in each column.

7	5	4						6	
		7	1		8				
4	9	2			3		1		
2					4			5	6
	1		2				7		4
	0		7	6					2
26	**18**	**28**	**35**	**29**	**31**	**21**	**23**	**29**	**30**

NUMBER LINK

Working from one square to another, horizontally or vertically (never diagonally), draw single continuous paths to pair up each set of two matching numbers.

No line may cross another, none may travel through any square containing a number, and every square must be visited just once.

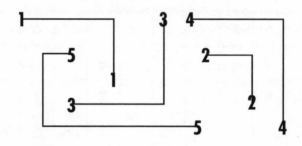

					10		9		5
	8		6		3		15		3
12				9	5		15		
	10	8							
			13						11
12		1				4	16		4
			13				7	11	
14	2			6		16		7	
2		1				14			

110

LIGHT UP

Place circles (representing light bulbs) in some of the empty squares, in such a way that no two bulbs shine on each other, until every square of the grid is lit up. A bulb sends rays of light horizontally and vertically, illuminating its entire row and column unless its light is blocked by a black cell.

Some black cells contain numbers, indicating how many light bulbs are in adjacent squares either immediately above, below, to the right, or to the left. Bulbs placed diagonally adjacent to a numbered cell do not contribute to the bulb count. An unnumbered black cell may have any number of light bulbs adjacent to it, or none at all, and not all light bulbs are necessarily clued via black squares.

SKYSCRAPERS

Place the numbers 1 to 7 into each row and column, one number per square. Each number represents a skyscraper of that many floors.

Arrange the skyscrapers in such a way that the given number outside the grid represents the number of buildings which can be seen from that point, looking only at that number's row or column.

A skyscraper with a lower number of floors cannot hide a higher building, but one with a higher number of floors always hides any building behind it.

	5	2	3	4	3	1		
							3	2
4					3			1
				1				3
2		4						2
2								5
1			6					
								2
	2	3	1	2	4	2		

112

COIN COLLECTING

In this puzzle, an amateur coin collector has been out with his metal detector, searching for booty. He didn't have time to dig up all the coins he found, so has made a grid map, showing their locations, in the hope that if he loses the map, at least no-one else will understand it... However, he didn't count on YOU coming across the strange grid (as seen here). Will you be able to discover the correct number of coins and their precise locations?

Those squares containing numbers are empty, but where a number appears in a square, it indicates how many coins are located in the squares (up to a maximum of eight) surrounding the numbered one, touching it at any corner or side. There is only one coin in any individual square.

Place a circle into every square containing a coin.

1	2	1						2		
					4		1		1	
2					5			1		
	4		6				2			2
1				5						4
1		4	5					4		
	2				4	4	4			2
		2		3			4	3	3	
		2			2	3				
2			3			3			4	
1					1			3		2

NO THREE IN LINE

Place either O or X into each empty square, so that no three consecutive squares in either a horizontal row or vertical column contain more than two of the same symbol.

There needs to be as many Os as Xs in every row and column.

			O	O				X	
		X		X			O	X	
	X				X				
O							O		
			X	X					X
X		X					O	X	
				O	O				O
	O				O				
				O				X	O
X	X		X						

COMBIKU

Each horizontal row and vertical column should contain
five different shapes, and five different numbers.

Every square will contain one number and one shape, and no combination
may be repeated anywhere else in the puzzle; so, for instance, if a square
contains a 3 and a star, then no other square containing a 3 will also
contain a star, and no other square with a star will also contain a 3.

1   **2**   **3**   **4**   **5**

LOGI-7

Every row and column of this grid should contain one
each of the letters A, B, C, D, E, F, and G.

In addition, each of the seven shapes (marked by thicker lines)
should also contain one each of the letters A, B, C, D, E, F, and G.

Can you complete the grid?

			F		C	
				D		
		G				
	F					E
						C
	A					
G		C			B	

SHAPE SORTER

The grid below is divided into regions of three squares.
Some need to contain three different shapes: a circle, a square,
and a triangle; others need to contain three identical shapes.

When two squares share a side across a region
boundary, the shapes must be different.

○   □   △

CHAINS

Fill each empty circle with one of the numbers 1-8.

Every horizontal row, vertical column, set of seven linked circles, and diagonal line of seven circles should contain seven different numbers.

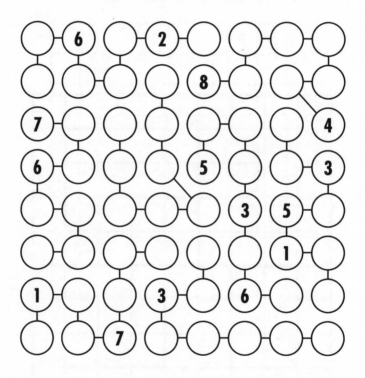

BRICKWORK

Every square should be filled with a number from 1 to 9.
No number may appear twice in any row or column.

Every brick that consists of two squares contains
both an odd number and an even number.

	6	8			1			
			6				7	
8		7			9			
	4					2		
		3	2			5	6	
					2	7		
	3					8		5
			8		5		9	
2			5					1

PATCHWORK

Every square should be filled with a letter from A to F, and each heavily outlined set of six squares should contain six different letters. Every row and column must contain two of each letter.

Squares that share a common border may not contain the same letter.

		E		B			B			F
A	F		E		C		F		B	
					F		B		B	D	E
	A		A		E		D			B	
					D			C			
E	F	C		F				B			C
				E		A			A	C	
	B					F		E		F	
		E	A			C		A			E
		D				D	E				
D	C		E				A	D	E	
B		D			F			E	F		

SLITHERLINK

Draw a single continuous loop, by connecting the
dots. No line may cross the path of another.

The figure inside each set of any four surrounding dots
indicates the total number of surrounding lines.

```
2       2  2       0  1  2  3

2  2  2       1             3

   3  1  3       0  1     1

   3

2       2  3  3     3     2  1

   2             3  2     1

         2             2

3     2  2     1       2  2

   1  1  3     3  3     1

      1     2     1     2  3

   3        1           3

2     1     3     1     3  2
```

CALCUDOKU

Each row and column should contain eight different numbers from 1 to 8.

The numbers placed in a heavily outlined set of squares may be repeated, but must produce the calculation in the top left corner, using the mathematical symbol provided: multiply (x), divide (/), add (+), and subtract (−).

For example, when multiplied, the numbers 4 and 3 total 12:

5−	13+		5+		12x		7/
	10x		42x		7+		
18+	3x		3/		15+		32x
	2/		1−	2−	10+		
	2/				7/		8+
24x	21+			12+	7+		
		11+			3/	7+	
2/			2−			2−	

BRIDGES

Join the circular islands by drawing horizontal or vertical lines to represent bridges, in such a way that the number of bridges connected to each island must match the number on that island. No bridge may cross another, and no more than two bridges can join any pair of islands.

The finished design will allow you to travel from one island to any other island on the map.

① ① ② ① ②

⑤ ④ ④ ② ③

① ④

① ③

③ ②

② ①

①

③ ⑥ ②

118

NO FOUR IN LINE

Place either O or X into each empty square, so that no four consecutive squares in a straight line in any direction (horizontally, vertically, or diagonally) contain more than three of the same symbol.

O							O	X	X	O	
		X							X	O	
	X	X	X			X	X			X	
	X				O			X			
	X						O				
	O	X		X		O					
O	X		X	X				O	O		
								O	O		
	O	O									
X											X
	X				O	X			X	X	
	X					O					
	O	O							X	O	

BATTLESHIPS

Can you place the vessels into the diagram? A number to the right or below a row or column refers to the number of occupied squares in that row or column.

Any vessel may be positioned horizontally or vertically, but no part of a vessel touches part of any other vessel, either horizontally, vertically, or diagonally.

Empty Area of Sea:

Aircraft Carrier:

Battleships:

Cruisers:

Submarines:

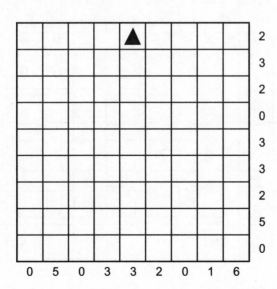

FUTOSHIKI

Fill the grid so that every horizontal row and vertical
column contains all the numbers 1 to 8.

Any arrows in the grid always point toward a square that contains a lower number.

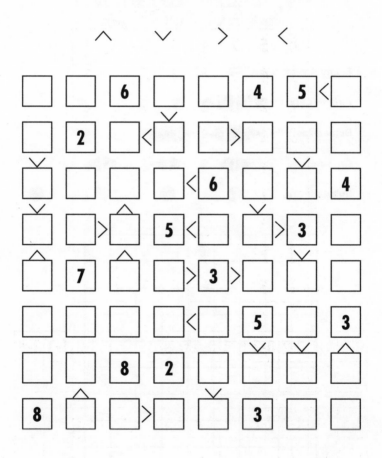

DOMINO PLACEMENT

121

A set of 36 dominoes has been laid out as shown.
Can you draw in the edges of them all?

The check-box is provided as an aid, so that you can
see which dominoes have been located.

0	5	2	4	4	0	7	1
1	4	0	6	3	3	3	5
7	2	0	2	2	5	5	7
3	4	1	5	6	2	4	6
6	1	0	3	4	4	0	0
6	1	7	4	2	5	7	1
5	3	5	7	3	5	0	6
4	7	2	1	6	2	1	6
1	3	2	6	0	7	7	3

0-0	0-1	0-2	0-3	0-4	0-5	0-6	0-7	1-1	1-2	1-3	1-4

1-5	1-6	1-7	2-2	2-3	2-4	2-5	2-6	2-7	3-3	3-4	3-5

3-6	3-7	4-4	4-5	4-6	4-7	5-5	5-6	5-7	6-6	6-7	7-7

HIDATO

Starting at 1 and finishing at 64, track your way from one square to another, either horizontally, vertically, or diagonally, placing consecutive numbers into the empty squares as you go.

19	18			28		36	
		22	31		35		37
6	21						
7	5	3			33	43	
		14	2	1			
		59				45	
	10		58		56		49
11	64			55		48	

SUM TOTAL

Fill each empty square so that every row contains ten different numbers from 0 to 9. In columns the numbers may be repeated, but wherever one square touches another, whether horizontally, vertically, or diagonally, the numbers must be different. Some are already in place.

The black squares show the sum total of the numbers in each column.

7		3	9			6			
4	0				9	3			7	8
9					6	4		2	5
	7		2	9	1		8		
					8	5	0	2	
4			8		7				5
33	**27**	**23**	**31**	**25**	**32**	**30**	**23**	**23**	**23**

129

124

NUMBER LINK

Working from one square to another, horizontally or vertically (never diagonally), draw single continuous paths to pair up each set of two matching numbers.

No line may cross another, none may travel through any square containing a number, and every square must be visited just once.

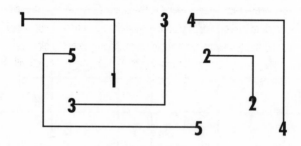

7			7	9					14
	11	1							
						16			
		5							
			13	2			2	13	
		5	9	16		4			
			1	6				12	10
						14			
	6	8	8	15			10	12	
					3				
11	15	3							4

LIGHT UP

Place circles (representing light bulbs) in some of the empty squares, in such a way that no two bulbs shine on each other, until every square of the grid is lit up. A bulb sends rays of light horizontally and vertically, illuminating its entire row and column unless its light is blocked by a black cell.

Some black cells contain numbers, indicating how many light bulbs are in adjacent squares either immediately above, below, to the right, or to the left. Bulbs placed diagonally adjacent to a numbered cell do not contribute to the bulb count. An unnumbered black cell may have any number of light bulbs adjacent to it, or none at all, and not all light bulbs are necessarily clued via black squares.

SKYSCRAPERS

Place the numbers 1 to 7 into each row and column, one number per square. Each number represents a skyscraper of that many floors.

Arrange the skyscrapers in such a way that the given number outside the grid represents the number of buildings which can be seen from that point, looking only at that number's row or column.

A skyscraper with a lower number of floors cannot hide a higher building, but one with a higher number of floors always hides any building behind it.

	3	2	2		4		
4	5						**2**
1							**2**
					4		**2**
		4					
3			3	1			**2**
4	2						**1**
2			1				**3**
	4	3	4			2	

COIN COLLECTING

In this puzzle, an amateur coin collector has been out with his metal detector, searching for booty. He didn't have time to dig up all the coins he found, so has made a grid map, showing their locations, in the hope that if he loses the map, at least no-one else will understand it... However, he didn't count on YOU coming across the strange grid (as seen here). Will you be able to discover the correct number of coins and their precise locations?

Those squares containing numbers are empty, but where a number appears in a square, it indicates how many coins are located in the squares (up to a maximum of eight) surrounding the numbered one, touching it at any corner or side. There is only one coin in any individual square.

Place a circle into every square containing a coin.

	2		1			2			1	1
		2			1			3		
1				3		2				
	2							1	3	3
3				4	4					
	2					2			2	
	2		2					4		
		4								1
						1		1		2
2	2		3		3			1		
1				1		1			2	1

NO THREE IN LINE

Place either O or X into each empty square, so that no three consecutive squares in either a horizontal row or vertical column contain more than two of the same symbol.

There needs to be as many Os as Xs in every row and column.

	O						X	X	
				X				X	
					O		O		
						O		X	
					X			X	
						O			O
X		O	X		X		X		
X		O	X					O	
X	X			O	X				

COMBIKU

Each horizontal row and vertical column should contain
five different shapes, and five different numbers.

Every square will contain one number and one shape, and no combination
may be repeated anywhere else in the puzzle; so, for instance, if a square
contains a 3 and a star, then no other square containing a 3 will also
contain a star, and no other square with a star will also contain a 3.

1   **2**   **3**   **4**   **5**

LOGI-7

Every row and column of this grid should contain one
each of the letters A, B, C, D, E, F, and G.

In addition, each of the seven shapes (marked by thicker lines)
should also contain one each of the letters A, B, C, D, E, F, and G.

Can you complete the grid?

F						
		E				G
	B			G	E	
				C		
		G		D		B
				E	D	
		D				

SHAPE SORTER

The grid below is divided into regions of three squares. Some need to contain three different shapes: a circle, a square, and a triangle; others need to contain three identical shapes.

When two squares share a side across a region boundary, the shapes must be different.

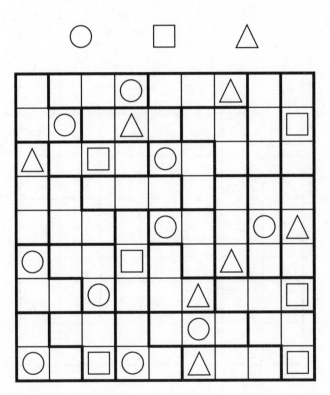

CHAINS

Fill each empty circle with one of the numbers 1-8.

Every horizontal row, vertical column, set of seven linked circles, and diagonal line of seven circles should contain seven different numbers.

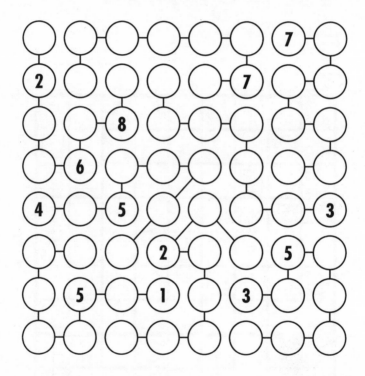

1

2	1	2	6	0	3	2
1	6	1	0	6	6	2
1	4	1	4	4	1	0
0	4	5	2	3	3	3
4	6	6	0	5	4	4
3	5	5	6	5	1	6
5	3	0	5	0	2	3
1	3	2	2	0	5	4

2

15	14	13	12	8	7	6
18	16	20	11	23	9	5
17	19	21	22	10	24	4
30	28	32	26	25	2	3
29	31	27	33	49	1	38
45	46	47	48	34	39	37
44	43	42	41	40	35	36

3

3	6	9	8	4	1	0	7	2	5
4	8	7	1	2	5	6	9	3	0
0	5	2	3	9	8	4	7	6	1
4	7	9	5	1	3	6	2	0	8
6	1	0	2	4	9	5	8	3	7
2	8	7	5	3	1	6	0	9	4
19	35	34	24	23	27	27	33	23	25

4

			8	18				11
8	4	3				12		12
5			18	2		13		13
					11	14		
		6	3				2	14
	6	17						17
1								
5	4			10		15	7	
10		9			1	9		
16			16				7	15

5

(grid puzzle with dots and numbers: 0, 1, 1, 3, 1, 3, 1)

6

5	3	4	6	1	2
4	5	6	3	2	1
1	6	3	2	4	5
6	2	1	5	3	4
2	1	5	4	6	3
3	4	2	1	5	6

7

●	2	●		●				●
1		1		2		2	●	2
	2	1	3	●	4	●	3	
●		●		●	●	3	●	1
	2		4	●			3	
2	2	1		●	3	●	2	●
●	●	3				2		2
3	●	4	●		1	●	2	●
	2	●						

8

O	O	X	X	O	X	O	X
O	X	O	O	X	X	O	X
X	O	X	O	X	O	X	O
O	O	X	X	O	O	X	X
X	X	O	O	X	X	O	O
O	O	X	O	X	O	X	X
X	X	O	X	O	O	X	O
X	X	O	X	O	X	O	O

9

⬡2	★3	◯1	☐4	◇5
◯4	☐5	◇2	⬡3	★1
★5	◯2	☐3	◇1	⬡4
◇3	⬡1	★4	◯5	☐2
☐1	◇4	⬡5	★2	◯3

10

E	D	F	A	B	C
C	B	A	F	E	D
D	F	C	B	A	E
B	C	D	E	F	A
A	E	B	D	C	F
F	A	E	C	D	B

11

◯	△	△	☐	◯	◯	◯	△
△	☐	△	☐	△	△	☐	△
☐	◯	◯	◯	△	◯	◯	△
☐	◯	△	△	△	◯	☐	◯
◯	△	☐	△	◯	△	◯	△
△	◯	△	◯	☐	◯	◯	☐
△	◯	◯	△	△	△	☐	☐
△	☐	△	◯	◯	◯	△	△
☐	☐	△	△	☐	☐	☐	△

12

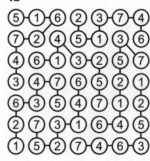

5	1	6	2	3	7	4
7	2	4	5	1	3	6
4	6	1	3	2	5	7
3	4	7	6	5	2	1
6	3	5	4	7	1	2
2	7	3	1	6	4	5
1	5	2	7	4	6	3

13

4	7	1	2	3	8	5	6
8	5	6	3	2	7	4	1
7	4	8	1	6	5	2	3
1	6	3	5	4	2	7	8
2	3	4	7	8	1	6	5
6	2	5	4	1	3	8	7
3	8	7	6	5	4	1	2
5	1	2	8	7	6	3	4

14

E	C	A	D	B	E	B	A	C	D
D	E	B	C	D	A	C	B	E	A
E	C	D	B	A	E	A	C	B	D
A	B	A	E	C	D	B	D	C	E
B	A	D	B	E	C	E	A	D	C
C	D	E	A	C	B	D	E	A	B
D	B	C	E	A	C	E	B	D	A
C	D	E	A	B	D	C	E	A	B
A	E	B	C	D	A	D	C	B	E
B	A	C	D	E	B	A	D	E	C

15

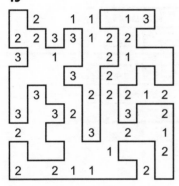

16

6	2	4	1	3	5
1	6	3	5	2	4
5	4	2	3	1	6
4	3	1	6	5	2
3	5	6	2	4	1
2	1	5	4	6	3

17

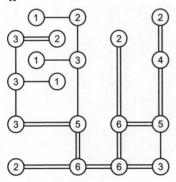

18

X	X	O	O	O	X	X	O	O	X
X	O	X	X	O	O	O	X	O	O
X	O	X	O	X	X	X	O	X	X
O	X	O	O	X	X	X	O	X	O
O	X	O	X	O	O	O	X	O	X
O	O	O	X	O	O	O	X	O	X
X	X	X	O	X	X	X	O	O	O
X	X	X	O	X	X	X	O	X	O
O	O	X	X	O	O	O	X	X	X
O	X	O	O	O	X	X	X	O	O
O	X	X	O	X	O	O	O	X	O

19

20

3	5	1	6	2	4	7
6	1	7	4	3	5	2
2	6	5	3	7	1	4
1	3	6	2	4	7	5
4	2	3	7	5	6	1
7	4	2	5	1	3	6
5	7	4	1	6	2	3

21

5	1	1	4	3	6	3
2	6	4	4	2	2	4
0	1	1	5	6	6	5
2	6	0	0	5	0	5
4	6	3	2	3	0	5
4	1	5	2	0	2	4
4	0	6	3	3	0	1
6	1	1	3	5	3	2

22

9	8	7	13	5	4	2
10	11	12	6	14	1	3
21	20	24	18	16	15	41
22	23	19	25	17	40	42
31	32	26	37	39	43	44
30	27	33	36	38	48	45
28	29	35	34	49	46	47

23

5	8	4	1	3	6	7	0	9	2
1	9	7	5	8	0	2	3	6	4
2	4	6	1	7	3	9	0	8	5
0	7	9	5	2	8	6	3	1	4
4	6	2	0	7	3	1	9	8	5
8	9	7	1	5	0	4	6	2	3
20	43	35	13	32	20	29	21	34	23

24

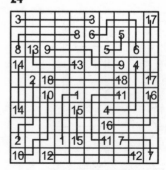

25

	●					
●	2				●	
			●	1		0
		●		0	1	0
		1	0		●	
	●					
	1			●	2	●

26

6	5	2	1	3	4
4	6	5	3	1	2
3	4	6	5	2	1
5	1	4	2	6	3
1	2	3	4	5	6
2	3	1	6	4	5

27

●	2	●	2	●	2		2	●
	4			2	3	●		1
●	2	●	2		●	3		1
				●	3	2	●	2
1	1			●			4	●
●		2	●	3		●	●	2
			●	4	4	●		
	2	4	●	●		●	5	●
	●	●	3			2	●	●

28

O	X	O	O	X	O	X	X
X	O	O	X	O	X	X	O
O	O	X	O	X	X	O	X
O	X	X	O	X	O	O	X
X	O	O	X	O	X	X	O
X	O	X	X	O	O	X	O
O	X	X	O	X	O	O	X
X	X	O	X	O	X	O	O

29

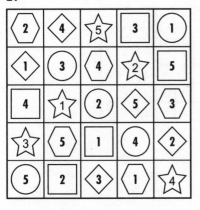

30

B	A	C	E	F	D
C	E	F	A	D	B
E	F	D	C	B	A
A	D	E	B	C	F
F	B	A	D	E	C
D	C	B	F	A	E

143

31

□ ○ ○ ○ □ □ □ △
□ △ □ □ ○ ○ ○ □
□ △ △ □ △ △ △ ○
△ □ ○ □ ○ □ ○ △
□ ○ □ ○ △ □ △ ○
□ △ △ △ □ △ □ △
□ ○ ○ ○ □ △ △ ○
○ △ △ △ □ ○ □ □
○ ○ □ ○ △ ○ ○ □

32

5 2 4 7 3 6 1
1 6 3 4 7 5 2
2 5 7 3 4 1 6
6 3 1 2 5 4 7
7 4 6 5 1 2 3
4 7 2 1 6 3 5
3 1 5 6 2 7 4

33

7	6	3	8	1	4	5	2
8	3	6	5	4	1	2	7
5	4	2	1	7	8	3	6
1	7	8	2	5	3	6	4
3	8	5	6	2	7	4	1
6	1	4	3	8	2	7	5
2	5	7	4	3	6	1	8
4	2	1	7	6	5	8	3

34

C	E	B	A	D	C	D	E	B	A
E	C	E	B	A	D	C	B	A	D
C	E	D	C	B	A	E	A	D	B
B	C	A	E	D	B	D	C	E	A
A	B	D	A	C	E	B	D	C	E
D	A	B	D	E	C	A	E	B	C
E	D	C	B	A	E	C	B	A	D
B	A	E	D	C	B	E	A	D	C
A	D	C	E	B	A	B	D	C	E
D	B	A	C	E	D	A	C	E	B

35

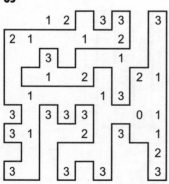

36

5	6	4	3	1	2
4	1	2	5	6	3
6	2	5	1	3	4
3	5	1	4	2	6
2	4	3	6	5	1
1	3	6	2	4	5

37

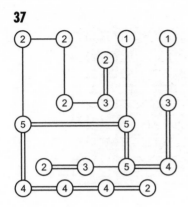

38

X	X	X	O	O	X	O	X	O	X
O	O	X	O	X	X	O	O	X	O
O	X	O	O	X	O	O	O	X	O
O	X	X	O	X	O	X	O	X	O
X	X	O	X	X	X	O	X	O	X
X	O	X	O	O	X	X	X	O	X
X	O	O	X	O	O	O	O	X	O
O	X	X	O	O	X	O	X	O	X
O	O	O	X	O	O	O	X	X	X
X	O	X	O	O	X	O	O	O	
O	O	X	X	O	X	O	X	O	X

39

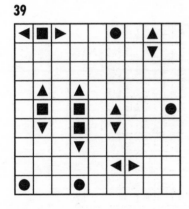

40

5	1	4	7	6	3	2
4	5	3	1	7	2	6
1	2	5	6	4	7	3
7	4	2	5	3	6	1
6	7	1	3	2	4	5
3	6	7	2	5	1	4
2	3	6	4	1	5	7

41

5	6	0	6	3	2	2
6	1	0	2	0	5	4
4	4	3	5	5	3	0
0	2	2	1	6	1	1
1	6	0	1	4	3	2
5	5	0	4	4	3	4
6	3	5	4	5	1	2
6	3	0	3	6	2	1

42

145

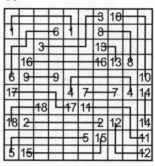

43

1	6	4	0	8	5	9	7	2	3
3	7	2	1	9	6	0	5	8	4
6	8	0	4	2	5	7	9	1	3
0	7	1	8	9	4	6	3	2	5
3	9	4	7	6	2	1	5	8	0
2	8	5	0	9	7	3	4	6	1
15	45	16	20	43	29	26	33	27	16

44

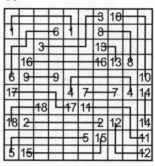

45

						●
	●		2	●		
●	3		●	3	●	
3	●				1	
●			2	●	1	
	0		●		1	●
		●				

46

3	5	1	4	2	6
6	1	4	2	3	5
2	6	5	1	4	3
1	2	6	3	5	4
4	3	2	5	6	1
5	4	3	6	1	2

47

●	2	●		●	3	●	3	●
2		2		2	5	●		2
●		●		●	4	●	4	●
●	4		4		3	●		
2	3	●	●	2		4	●	1
●	3	3		2	●	●	3	
2		●	1			4	●	1
●		2			●		3	
1	2	●		1	1		●	●

48

X	O	O	X	O	O	X	X
O	X	X	O	X	X	O	O
O	O	X	O	X	O	X	X
X	O	O	X	O	X	X	O
O	X	X	O	X	X	O	O
O	X	X	O	X	O	O	X
X	O	O	X	O	O	X	X
X	X	O	X	O	X	O	O

49

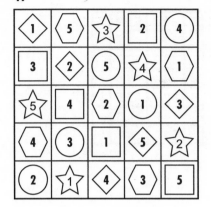

50

C	D	F	B	A	E
A	B	E	F	D	C
F	E	A	C	B	D
E	C	D	A	F	B
B	A	C	D	E	F
D	F	B	E	C	A

51

△	△	△	○	△	○	□	□
○	□	○	△	□	○	△	□
□	○	△	○	△	△	□	○
△	○	○	□	○	□	△	△
□	△	△	□	△	○	△	△
△	□	○	△	○	○	□	□
△	△	○	○	△	△	○	□
□	○	□	△	○	□	△	△
□	□	○	□	△	○	○	○

52

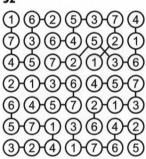

53

7	8	1	6	3	2	5	4
8	3	2	5	6	7	4	1
6	7	8	1	4	3	2	5
1	6	5	8	7	4	3	2
4	1	6	7	2	5	8	3
3	2	7	4	5	1	6	8
5	4	3	2	1	8	7	6
2	5	4	3	8	6	1	7

54

A	B	A	E	C	D	B	D	E	C
E	D	E	D	B	A	C	A	C	B
C	E	C	B	D	E	A	B	D	A
B	C	B	E	A	C	D	E	A	D
D	A	D	A	C	B	E	C	B	E
A	E	C	B	D	A	D	E	C	B
B	D	E	C	A	B	A	D	E	C
D	C	B	A	E	D	E	C	B	A
E	A	D	C	B	E	C	B	A	D
C	B	A	D	E	C	B	A	D	E

147

55

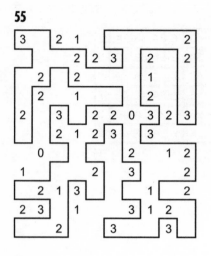

56

5	7	3	1	6	4	2
2	1	4	5	3	7	6
6	5	7	3	4	2	1
3	6	2	4	1	5	7
1	4	5	7	2	6	3
7	2	1	6	5	3	4
4	3	6	2	7	1	5

57

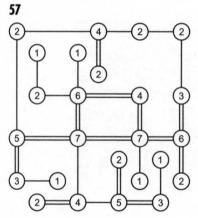

58

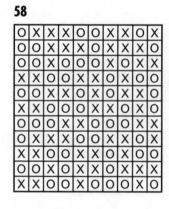

59

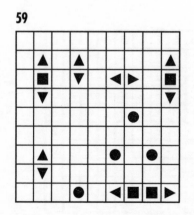

60

2	4	7	3	5	6	1
5	7	6	4	1	3	2
3	5	4	1	7	2	6
6	3	1	2	4	5	7
1	6	2	7	3	4	5
7	2	3	5	6	1	4
4	1	5	6	2	7	3

61

5	6	5	5	2	5	0
2	1	3	6	2	4	6
5	2	3	6	4	4	1
1	6	0	0	2	5	4
0	4	3	0	1	0	2
3	3	2	1	6	5	0
2	1	4	4	4	1	3
0	1	5	3	3	6	6

62

39	40	35	34	33	28	27
41	38	43	36	32	26	29
17	42	37	44	25	31	30
18	16	21	24	45	49	47
19	20	15	22	23	46	48
3	1	5	14	8	9	10
2	4	6	7	13	12	11

63

7	3	8	1	5	2	4	9	0	6
4	0	9	3	8	6	5	2	1	7
7	1	2	5	4	0	3	6	9	8
8	9	0	3	6	7	1	5	2	4
6	1	7	8	4	2	3	0	9	5
8	9	4	1	3	0	7	5	6	2
40	23	30	21	30	17	23	27	27	32

64

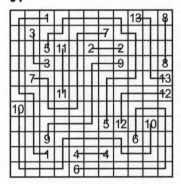

65

66

5	2	1	4	3	6
4	5	2	6	1	3
2	1	3	5	6	4
1	6	4	3	5	2
6	3	5	2	4	1
3	4	6	1	2	5

67

1	1	1	2	●	2	●	●	2
●	2		●		3		●	3
3	●	3		3	●	4	●	2
2	●			●	5	●	3	
3	3		●	4	●	●		2
●	●	5	●			4	●	●
3	●	●	4	●	2	●		2
	3		●	3				1
●		1		2	●		1	●

68

X	O	O	X	O	X	X	O
O	O	X	O	X	O	X	X
O	X	O	O	X	X	O	X
X	O	X	X	O	O	X	O
O	X	O	O	X	X	O	X
O	X	X	O	X	O	O	X
X	O	X	X	O	O	X	O
X	X	O	X	O	X	O	O

69

5 ◇	3 ☆	2 ▢	4 ○	1 ⬡
2 ☆	1 ○	3 ⬡	5 ▢	4 ◇
4 ⬡	2 ◇	5 ○	1 ☆	3 ▢
1 ▢	5 ⬡	4 ☆	3 ◇	2 ○
3 ○	4 ▢	1 ◇	2 ⬡	5 ☆

70

A	C	E	D	F	B
D	B	F	E	C	A
C	E	B	A	D	F
F	A	D	C	B	E
E	F	C	B	A	D
B	D	A	F	E	C

71

○	▢	▢	○	○	△	▢	▢
○	○	▢	△	○	△	△	▢
▢	△	△	○	△	○	○	○
▢	▢	△	△	○	△	▢	▢
△	○	○	△	▢	△	△	▢
△	△	○	△	△	▢	○	○
○	▢	△	▢	○	▢	▢	○
○	▢	▢	○	△	○	△	▢
○	△	△	△	▢	△	▢	○

72

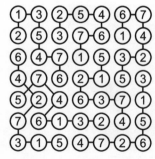

150

73

8	7	5	4	2	3	1	6
4	1	8	6	3	2	7	5
2	3	6	7	4	1	5	8
7	5	4	1	6	8	3	2
5	8	3	2	1	4	6	7
3	6	1	8	5	7	2	4
1	4	2	5	7	6	8	3
6	2	7	3	8	5	4	1

74

B	A	E	C	D	B	D	E	A	C
C	B	D	A	C	E	A	D	B	E
B	A	C	D	E	B	E	A	D	C
E	D	E	B	A	C	D	C	A	B
D	E	C	D	B	A	B	E	C	A
A	C	B	E	A	D	C	B	E	D
C	D	A	B	E	A	B	D	C	E
A	C	B	E	D	C	A	B	E	D
E	B	D	A	C	E	C	A	D	B
D	E	A	C	B	D	E	C	B	A

75

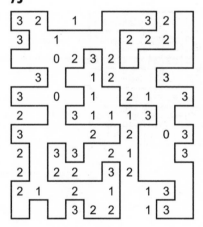

76

2	4	1	5	6	7	3
5	2	7	1	4	3	6
1	5	4	7	3	6	2
7	3	2	6	1	5	4
4	6	5	3	2	1	7
6	1	3	4	7	2	5
3	7	6	2	5	4	1

77

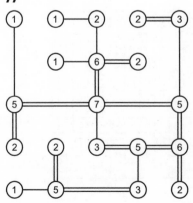

78

X	X	O	O	O	X	X	O	O	O
O	O	X	O	O	O	X	O	X	O
X	O	O	O	X	X	O	O	O	X
O	X	X	X	O	X	X	X	O	O
X	O	X	O	X	X	O	O	X	X
O	O	X	O	X	O	O	X	O	X
X	X	O	O	O	X	X	O	O	O
X	O	X	X	O	X	O	X	O	O
X	O	O	X	X	O	X	O	O	O
O	X	O	O	O	X	O	X	O	X
O	O	X	X	X	O	O	O	X	O

79

80

6	4	3	2	7	1	5
4	5	6	3	2	7	1
3	6	7	1	4	5	2
2	3	5	4	1	6	7
1	2	4	7	5	3	6
7	1	2	5	6	4	3
5	7	1	6	3	2	4

81

2	3	2	2	5	4	4
5	3	6	1	0	3	6
5	3	0	3	5	2	1
2	0	0	6	0	5	5
4	4	5	0	3	4	5
2	3	0	6	1	1	6
2	1	4	6	2	4	1
3	6	1	6	1	4	0

82

28	29	30	31	32	42	41
27	23	24	33	43	45	40
26	25	22	34	44	39	46
18	21	36	35	38	47	49
17	19	20	37	2	3	48
15	16	12	10	9	1	4
14	13	11	8	7	6	5

83

7	8	4	6	5	2	0	1	3	9
9	2	7	0	1	3	5	4	8	6
8	5	3	6	7	9	0	1	2	4
7	1	4	2	8	6	5	3	0	9
8	5	9	1	7	3	0	4	6	2
3	4	6	0	5	2	1	7	9	8
42	25	33	15	33	25	11	20	28	38

84

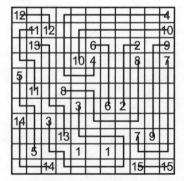

85

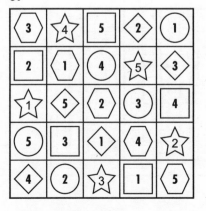

86

4	3	6	1	2	5
2	4	5	6	3	1
6	5	4	3	1	2
5	1	3	2	4	6
1	6	2	4	5	3
3	2	1	5	6	4

87

88

X	X	O	O	X	O	O	X
X	O	X	O	O	X	X	O
O	X	O	X	O	O	X	X
O	O	X	O	X	X	O	X
X	O	X	X	O	O	X	O
O	X	O	X	X	O	X	O
O	O	X	O	X	X	O	X
X	X	O	X	O	X	O	O

89

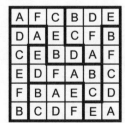

90

A	F	C	B	D	E
D	A	E	C	F	B
C	E	B	D	A	F
E	D	F	A	B	C
F	B	A	E	C	D
B	C	D	F	E	A

91

□	△	△	△	□	□	△	○	□
□	□	○	○	□	△	○	□	○
○	△	○	○	△	□	△	○	△
□	△	△	□	○	△	○	△	□
△	○	□	○	△	○	△	□	○
□	△	○	△	□	△	△	△	○
△	○	□	○	△	□	○	□	○
○	□	△	○	□	□	△	○	△
△	○	□	○	△	□	○	△	△

92

5	7	6	4	2	8	3	1
8	4	5	6	1	3	2	7
1	8	2	3	7	4	6	5
2	6	3	1	5	7	4	8
3	1	4	7	8	2	5	6
7	5	8	2	3	6	1	4
4	3	1	8	6	5	7	2
6	2	7	5	4	1	8	3

93

4	9	3	6	8	1	7	2	5
9	8	7	1	2	5	6	3	4
2	3	5	4	6	7	1	8	9
1	4	9	8	5	3	2	7	6
8	5	4	3	1	2	9	6	7
7	6	1	2	3	9	4	5	8
3	2	8	7	9	6	5	4	1
5	7	6	9	4	8	3	1	2
6	1	2	5	7	4	8	9	3

94

D	E	C	B	F	A	E	D	C	B	F	A
E	A	D	C	B	F	D	C	A	E	B	F
D	E	C	F	D	B	A	E	C	B	F	A
E	A	E	D	B	C	F	D	B	C	A	F
C	D	A	B	F	E	C	B	A	F	D	E
B	C	F	A	E	D	B	F	E	A	C	D
F	D	A	F	C	B	E	A	D	E	B	C
A	C	B	A	E	F	D	C	F	D	E	B
C	B	F	D	A	E	B	E	D	F	A	C
B	F	D	E	C	A	C	A	F	D	E	B
F	B	E	C	A	D	F	B	E	A	C	D
A	F	B	E	D	C	A	F	B	C	D	E

95

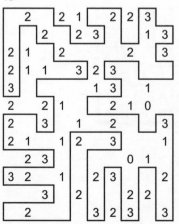

96

7	2	5	6	4	3	1	8
8	7	4	2	6	1	5	3
2	3	1	5	7	8	6	4
5	1	6	4	8	7	3	2
3	6	2	8	5	4	7	1
4	5	7	1	3	2	8	6
1	8	3	7	2	6	4	5
6	4	8	3	1	5	2	7

97

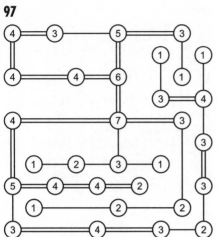

98

O	O	X	O	X	X	O	X	O	X
O	X	O	X	O	O	O	X	X	O
X	X	X	O	O	X	X	O	X	X
O	O	X	X	X	O	O	X	O	X
O	X	X	X	O	X	O	O	O	X
X	X	O	X	O	O	X	X	X	O
O	O	X	O	O	O	X	O	X	X
O	X	O	X	X	O	O	O	X	
O	X	O	O	O	X	O	X	O	X
X	X	O	X	O	X	X	O	O	
X	O	X	X	X	O	O	X	O	
X	X	O	X	O	O	O	X	X	X
O	X	O	O	X	X	O	X	O	X

99

100

7	4	5	8	2	6	3	1
1	6	3	2	7	4	5	8
3	1	2	7	5	8	4	6
6	2	4	3	1	7	8	5
2	3	1	4	8	5	6	7
8	5	6	1	4	2	7	3
4	8	7	5	6	3	1	2
5	7	8	6	3	1	2	4

101

1	7	1	6	3	1	0	0
0	2	5	4	5	6	7	1
1	0	6	7	5	3	3	1
4	3	6	2	5	4	2	3
5	1	3	7	6	4	6	2
1	4	1	2	7	0	6	0
6	4	5	3	7	7	2	3
7	0	5	5	7	0	0	4
4	3	4	2	6	2	2	5

102

34	33	28	29	8	9	13	11
32	35	30	27	7	14	10	12
36	31	26	4	15	6	17	19
37	25	3	23	5	16	20	18
38	2	24	51	22	21	64	61
1	39	49	50	52	63	62	60
40	42	45	48	53	56	57	59
41	43	44	46	47	54	55	58

103

7	5	4	9	8	0	1	3	6	2
3	0	6	7	1	2	8	4	5	9
4	9	2	8	5	6	3	0	1	7
2	0	7	1	3	9	4	8	5	6
6	1	9	2	5	8	0	7	3	4
4	3	0	8	7	6	5	1	9	2
26	18	28	35	29	31	21	23	29	30

104

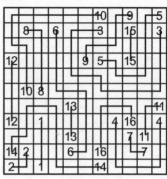

105

106

2	6	1	4	5	7	3
4	5	2	1	6	3	7
5	2	7	3	1	6	4
6	4	3	2	7	1	5
3	7	6	5	2	4	1
7	1	4	6	3	5	2
1	3	5	7	4	2	6

107

108

O	O	X	O	O	X	X	O	X	X
O	O	X	O	X	O	X	O	X	X
X	X	O	X	O	X	O	X	O	O
O	O	X	O	O	X	X	O	X	X
O	X	O	X	X	O	O	X	O	X
X	O	X	O	X	X	O	O	X	O
X	X	O	X	O	O	X	X	O	O
O	O	X	O	X	O	X	X	O	X
X	X	O	X	O	X	O	O	X	O
X	X	O	X	X	O	O	X	O	O

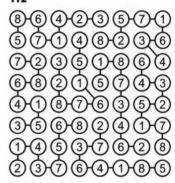

109

☆5	⬡2	○4	◇1	▢3
○2	◇3	⬡1	▢5	☆4
◇4	☆1	▢2	○3	⬡5
▢1	○5	☆3	⬡4	◇2
⬡3	▢4	◇5	☆2	○1

110

E	G	D	F	A	C	B
A	B	E	C	D	G	F
F	C	G	B	E	D	A
D	F	B	G	C	A	E
B	D	A	E	G	F	C
C	A	F	D	B	E	G
G	E	C	A	F	B	D

111

(shape logic grid)

112

8	6	4	2	3	5	7	1
5	7	1	4	8	2	3	6
7	2	3	5	1	8	6	4
6	8	2	1	5	7	4	3
4	1	8	7	6	3	5	2
3	5	6	8	2	4	1	7
1	4	5	3	7	6	2	8
2	3	7	6	4	1	8	5

113

5	6	8	3	2	1	9	4	7
1	8	9	6	5	3	4	7	2
8	5	7	4	6	9	1	2	3
9	4	5	1	8	7	2	3	6
4	7	3	2	1	8	5	6	9
3	1	6	9	4	2	7	5	8
6	3	2	7	9	4	8	1	5
7	2	1	8	3	5	6	9	4
2	9	4	5	7	6	3	8	1

114

C	A	E	F	B	D	A	C	B	D	E	F
A	F	B	E	D	C	E	F	C	A	B	D
F	C	A	D	E	F	C	B	A	B	D	E
C	A	F	A	C	E	B	D	F	E	B	D
A	D	A	C	B	D	F	E	C	F	E	B
E	F	C	B	F	A	E	D	B	D	A	C
B	E	F	D	E	B	A	C	D	A	C	F
D	B	C	B	D	E	F	A	E	C	F	A
F	D	E	A	C	B	C	F	A	B	D	E
E	B	D	F	A	C	D	E	F	C	A	B
D	C	B	E	F	A	B	A	D	E	F	C
B	E	D	C	A	F	D	B	E	F	C	A

115

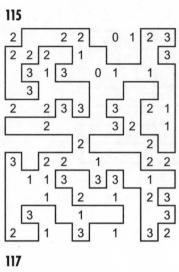

116

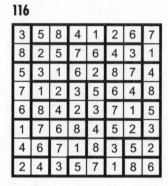

117

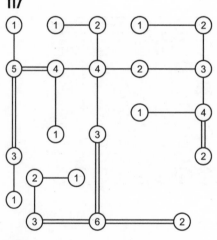

118

O	X	O	O	X	O	O	X	O
X	O	X	O	O	X	O	X	O
O	X	X	O	X	X	X	O	X
O	O	X	O	O	O	X	X	X
X	X	O	O	X	X	O	O	O
O	O	X	X	O	O	X	O	X
O	X	O	X	X	X	O	O	X
O	X	O	O	O	X	X	O	O
X	O	X	O	O	X	O	X	X
X	O	X	O	X	X	X	O	X
X	X	O	O	X	O	X	O	X
O	X	X	O	X	O	O	X	O
X	O	O	O	X	X	O	X	O

119

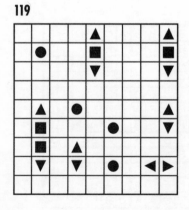

120

3	1	6	7	2	4	5	8
5	2	3	4	7	6	8	1
2	5	1	3	6	8	7	4
1	6	4	5	8	7	3	2
4	7	5	8	3	2	1	6
7	8	2	1	4	5	6	3
6	3	8	2	5	1	4	7
8	4	7	6	1	3	2	5

121

0	5	2	4	4	0	7	1
1	4	0	6	3	3	3	5
7	2	0	2	2	5	5	7
3	4	1	5	6	2	4	6
6	1	0	3	4	4	0	0
6	1	7	4	2	5	7	1
5	3	5	7	3	5	0	6
4	7	2	1	6	2	1	6
1	3	2	6	0	7	7	3

122

19	18	30	29	28	27	36	38
20	17	22	31	26	35	39	37
6	21	16	23	32	25	34	40
7	5	3	15	24	33	43	41
8	4	14	2	1	44	51	42
9	13	59	60	57	52	45	50
12	10	61	58	53	56	46	49
11	64	63	62	55	54	48	47

123

7	2	3	9	0	1	6	8	5	4
4	0	6	2	5	9	3	1	7	8
9	8	1	3	7	6	4	0	2	5
6	7	5	2	9	1	3	8	4	0
3	9	6	7	4	8	5	0	2	1
4	1	2	8	0	7	9	6	3	5
33	27	23	31	25	32	30	23	23	23

124

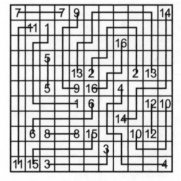

125

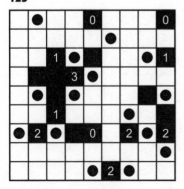

126

1	5	3	6	7	2	4
7	3	2	5	4	1	6
3	6	7	1	2	4	5
6	7	4	2	3	5	1
5	4	6	3	1	7	2
2	1	5	4	6	3	7
4	2	1	7	5	6	3

127

●2●1 ●2● 1 1
2 1 3 ●
1 ●3 2 ●●
●2 ●●● 1 3 3
3● ●4 4 ●
●2 ● 2 ●● 2
2 2 ●4
●4● ● 1
● ●● 1 1 2
2 2 3●3● 1 ●
1● 1 1 ●2 1

128

O	O	X	O	X	X	O	X	X	O
O	O	X	O	X	O	X	O	X	X
X	X	O	X	O	O	X	O	O	X
O	O	X	O	X	O	X	O	X	O
O	O	X	O	O	X	X	O	X	X
X	X	O	X	X	O	O	X	O	O
X	X	O	X	O	X	O	X	O	O
O	O	X	O	X	O	X	O	X	X
X	X	O	X	O	O	X	O	O	X
X	X	O	X	O	X	O	X	O	O

129

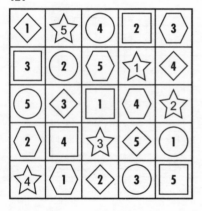

130

F	G	C	E	A	B	D
C	D	E	A	B	F	G
A	B	F	D	G	E	C
D	E	A	B	C	G	F
E	A	G	F	D	C	B
G	F	B	C	E	D	A
B	C	D	G	F	A	E

131

(grid of circle / triangle / square symbols, 9×9)

132

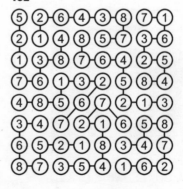

5	2	6	4	3	8	7	1
2	1	4	8	5	7	3	6
1	3	8	7	6	4	2	5
7	6	1	3	2	5	8	4
4	8	5	6	7	2	1	3
3	4	7	2	1	6	5	8
6	5	2	1	8	3	4	7
8	7	3	5	4	1	6	2